JACKIE CHAN
ADVENTURES

成龍歷險記

TOKYOPOP®

Los Angeles • Tokyo • London

Contributing Editors - Amy Court-Kaemon & Paul Morrissey
Copy Editors - Bryce Coleman & Tim Beedle
Graphic Design & Lettering - Rob Steen
Cover Layout - Aaron Suhr
Graphic Artist - Tomás Montalvo-Lagos

Editor - Elizabeth Hurchalla
Managing Editor - Jill Freshney
Production Manager - Antonio DePietro
Production Manager - Jennifer Miller
Art Director - Matt Alford
Editorial Director - Jeremy Ross
VP of Production - Ron Klamert
President & C.O.O. - John Parker
Publisher & C.E.O. - Stuart Levy

Email: editor@TOKYOPOP.com
Come visit us online at www.TOKYOPOP.com

A ⊙ **TOKYOPOP** Cine-Manga™
TOKYOPOP Inc.
5900 Wilshire Blvd., Suite 2000, Los Angeles, CA 90036

Jackie Chan Adventures Volume 2
TM & © 2004 Adelaide Productions, Inc. All Rights Reserved.
www.jackiechanadventures.com

ISBN: 1-59182-403-6

First TOKYOPOP printing: January 2004

10 9 8 7 6 5 4 3 2 1

Printed in China

JACKIE CHAN ADVENTURES™

LEGEND OF THE ZODIAC

CONTENTS

An expert in ancient artifacts, Jackie travels the world to find remnants of lost civilizations. Also a top martial artist, Jackie would always rather outwit his opponents than fight them. But when it's his only choice, Jackie can move faster than the eye can see.

JACKIE

Feisty, quick and smart, Jackie's niece Jade is the perfect addition to her uncle's crime-fighting team. At least, she thinks so.

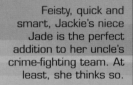

JADE

The most famous wrestler in all of Mexico, the legendary El Toro Fuerte is the mightiest of men.

EL TORO FUERTE

A young boy who dreams of someday being a star wrestler like his idol, El Toro Fuerte.

PACO

A fierce and beautiful cat burglar, Viper has no trouble matching Jackie's martial arts moves.

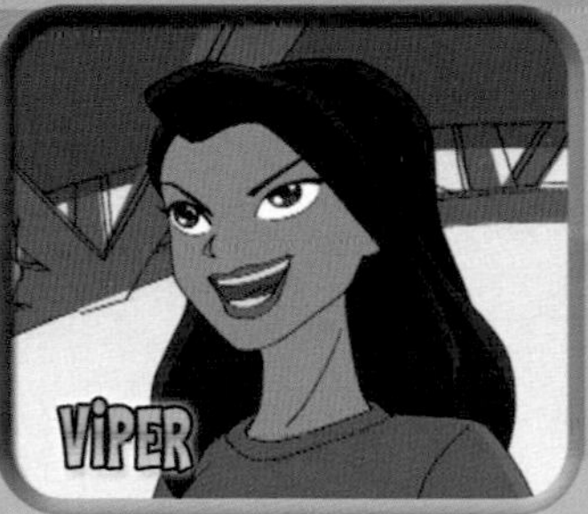
VIPER

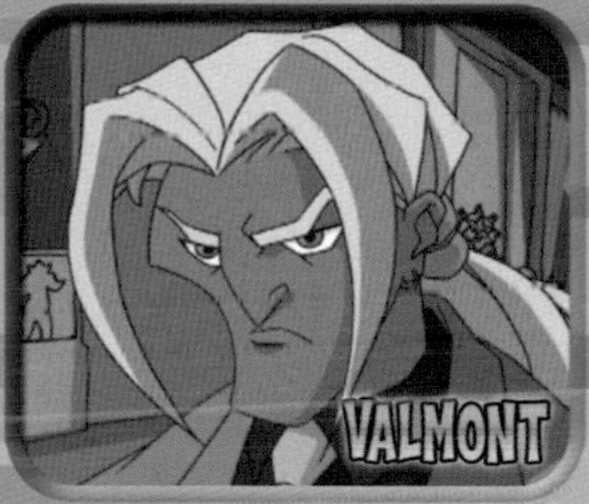
VALMONT

The leader of a powerful crime syndicate called the Dark Hand, Valmont needs to collect twelve magical talismans in order to free Shendu, the Fire Demon.

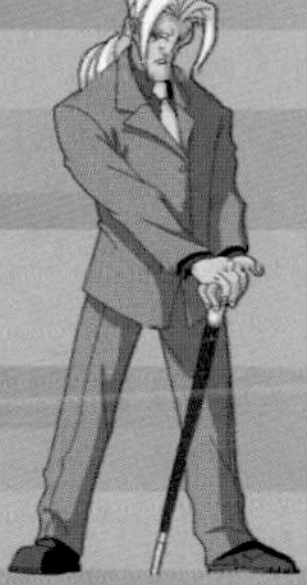

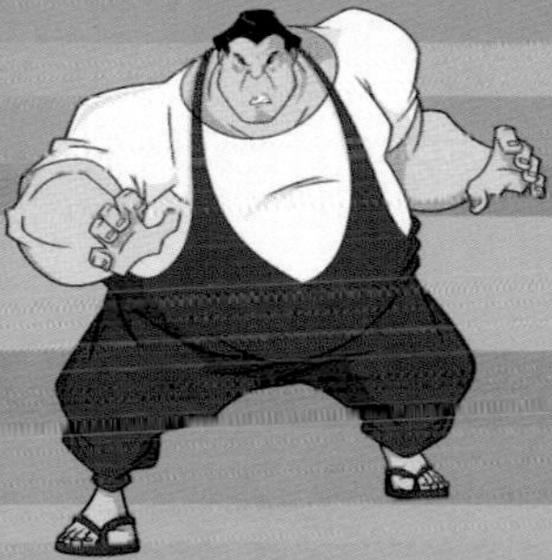

The main enforcer of the Dark Hand, Tohru the giant is literally Jackie's biggest threat.

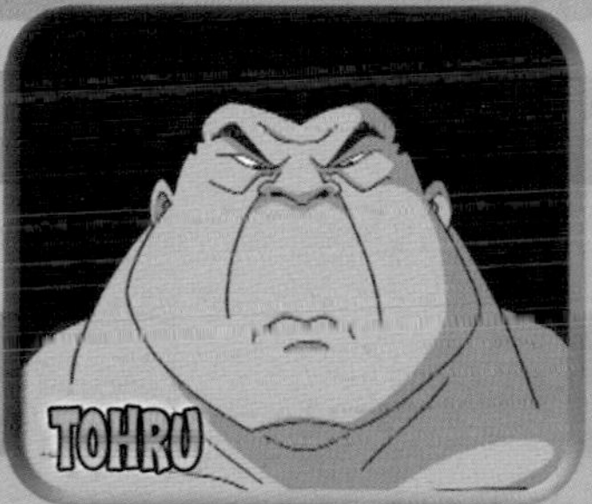
TOHRU

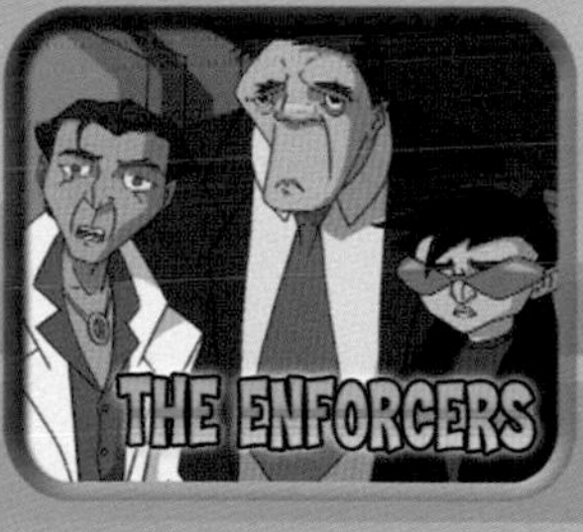
THE ENFORCERS

The Dark Hand's team of thugs. Finn, Chow and Ratso report to Valmont.

A team of supernatural black-clad warriors, the Shadowkhan are endless in number and fierce in skill.

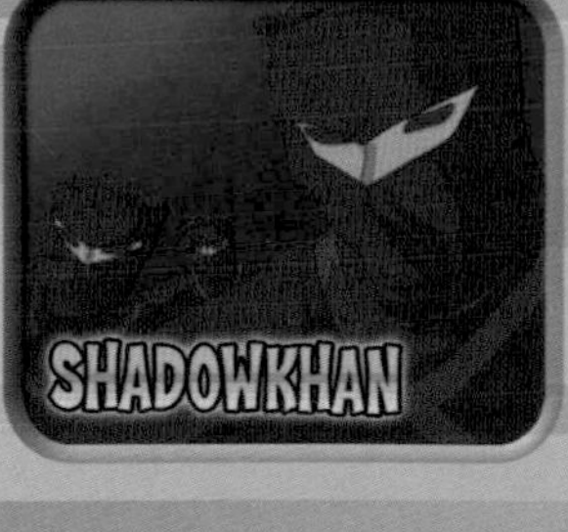
SHADOWKHAN

JACKIE CHAN ADVENTURES™

THE MASK OF EL TORO FUERTE

WRITTEN BY
DUANE CAPIZZI

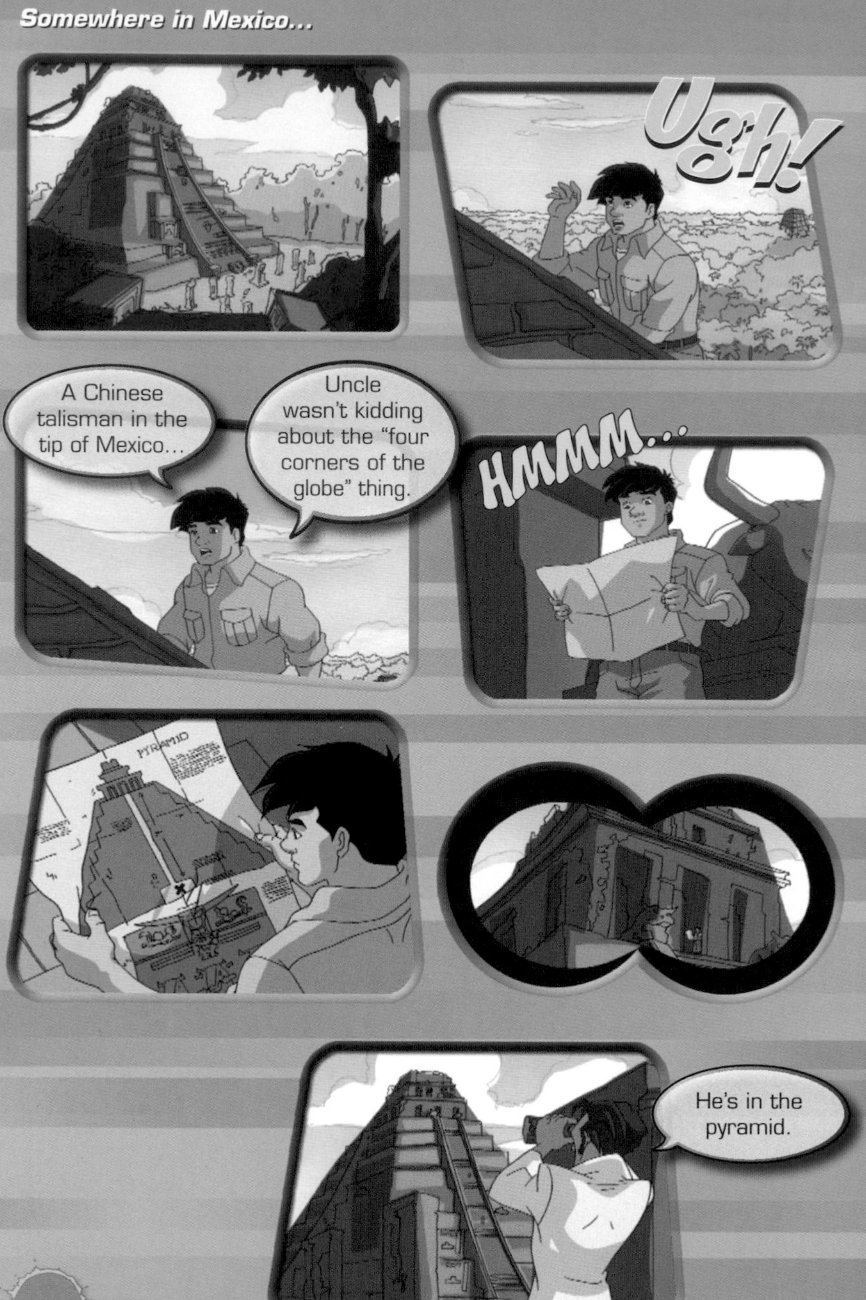
Somewhere in Mexico...
Ugh!
A Chinese talisman in the tip of Mexico...
Uncle wasn't kidding about the "four corners of the globe" thing.
HMMM...
PYRAMID
He's in the pyramid.

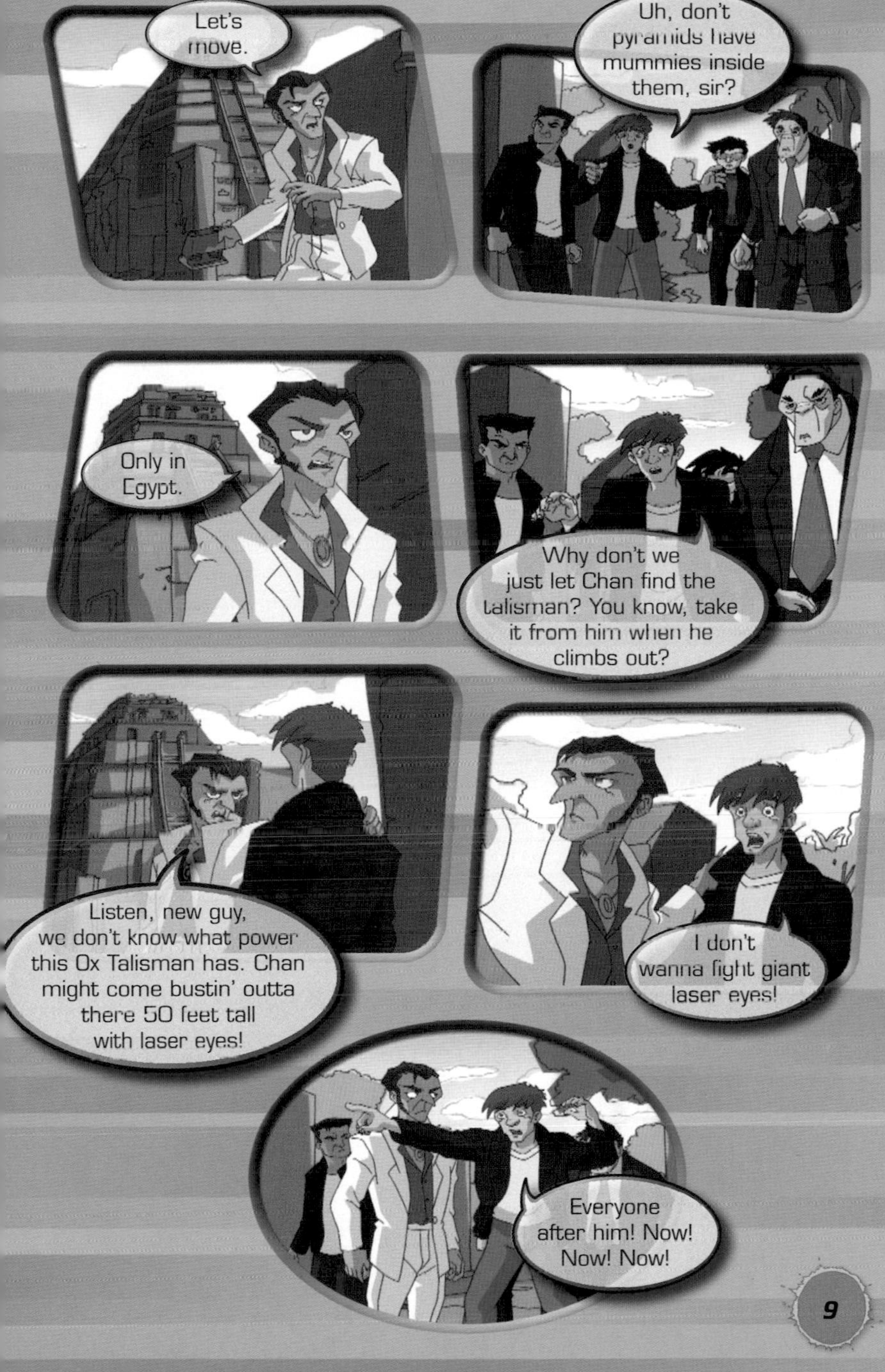
Let's move.
Uh, don't pyramids have mummies inside them, sir?
Only in Egypt.
Why don't we just let Chan find the talisman? You know, take it from him when he climbs out?
Listen, new guy, we don't know what power this Ox Talisman has. Chan might come bustin' outta there 50 feet tall with laser eyes!
I don't wanna fight giant laser eyes!
Everyone after him! Now! Now! Now!

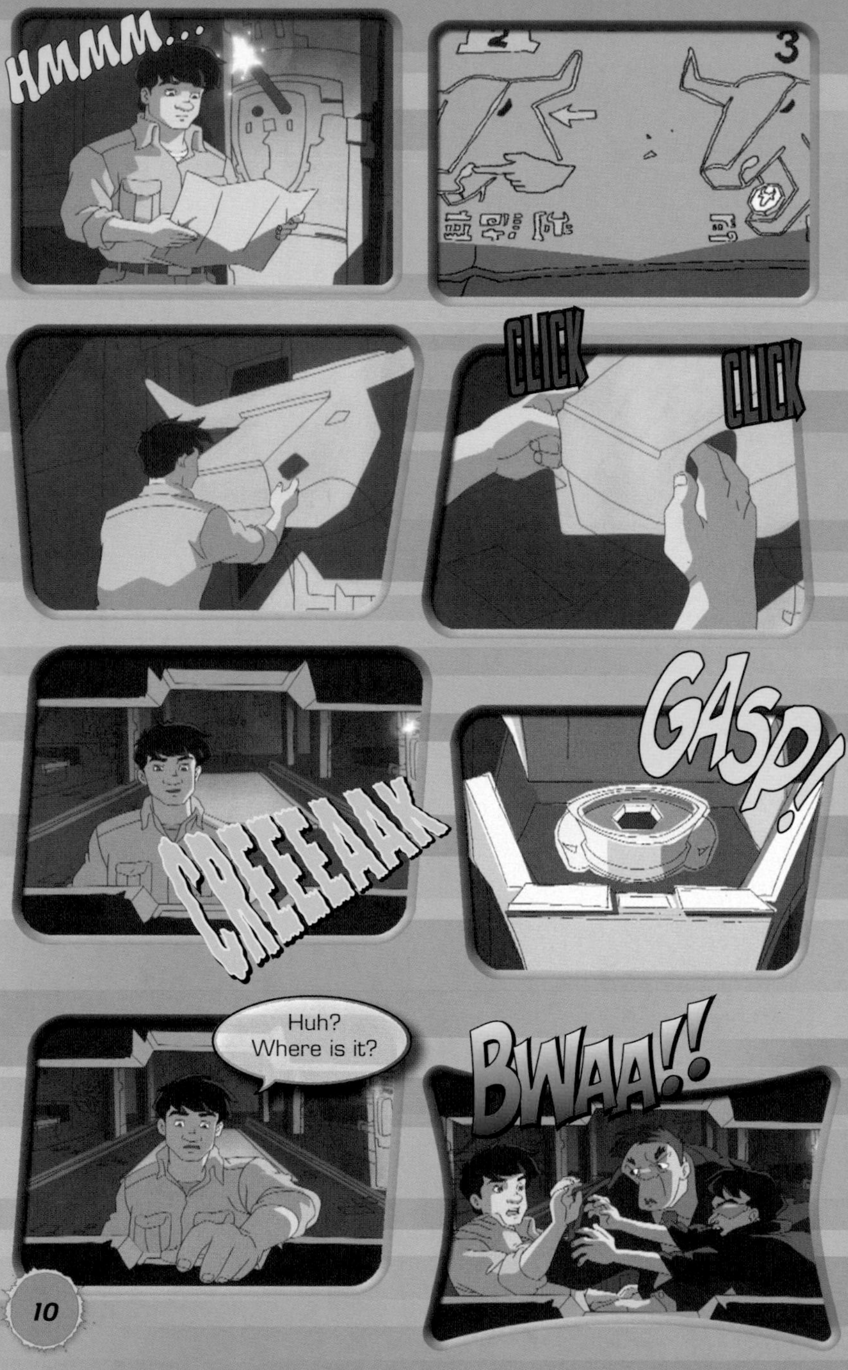
HMMM...
CLICK
CLICK
CREEEAAK
GASP!
Huh?
Where is it?
BWAA!!

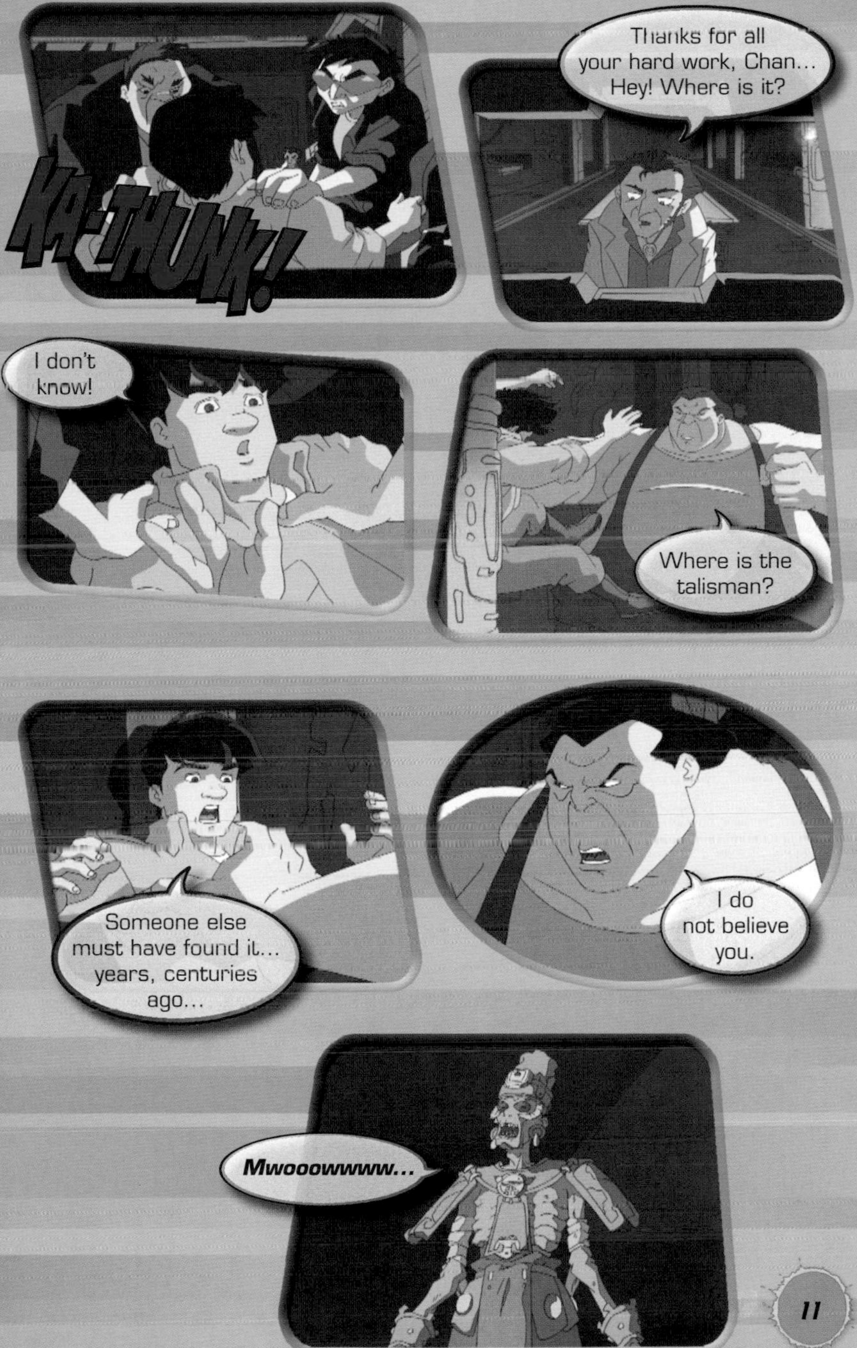
KA-THUNK!
Thanks for all your hard work, Chan... Hey! Where is it?
I don't know!
Where is the talisman?
Someone else must have found it... years, centuries ago...
I do not believe you.
Mwooowwww...

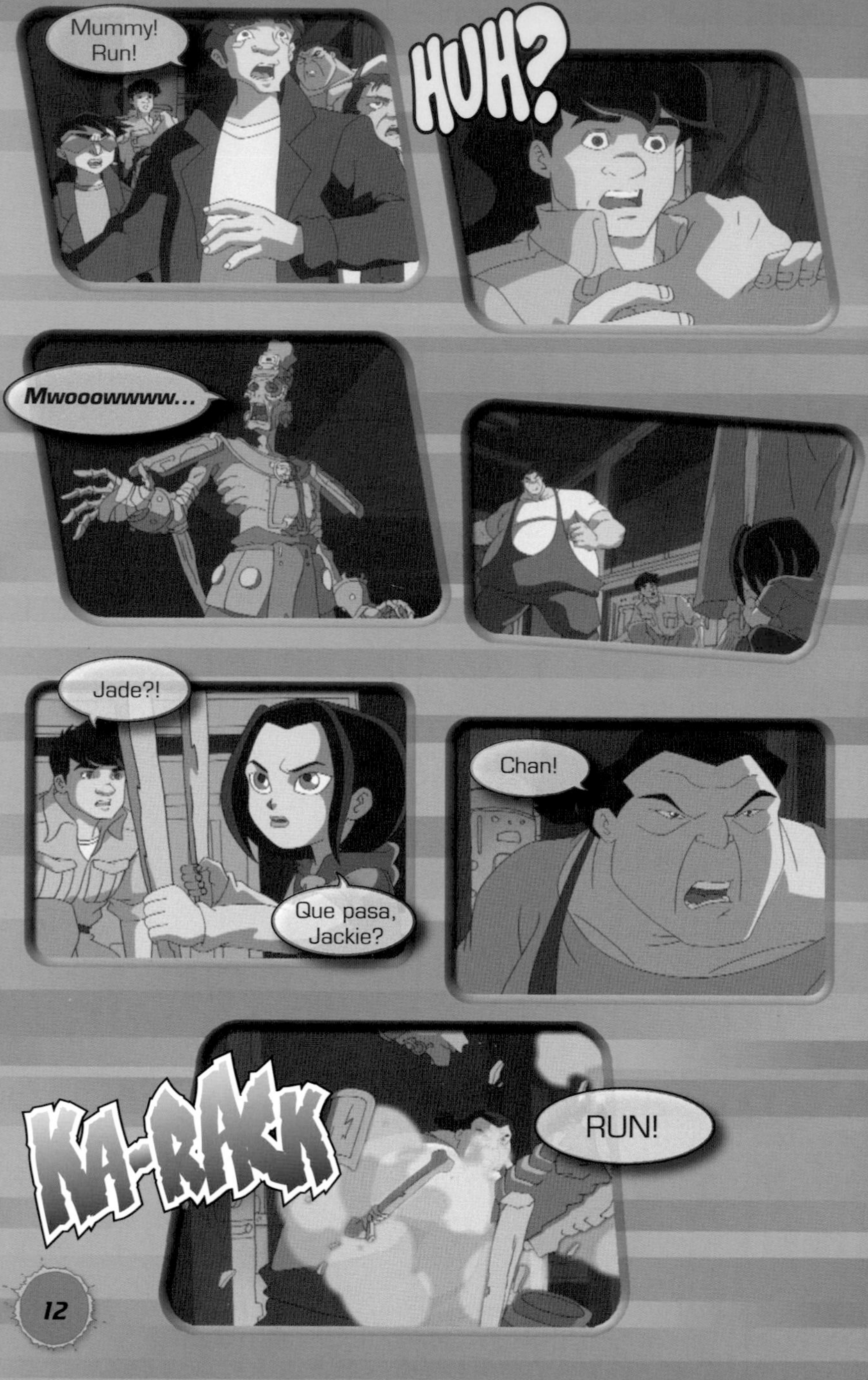
Mummy! Run!
HUH?
Mwooowwww...
Jade?!
Que pasa, Jackie?
Chan!
KA-RACK
RUN!

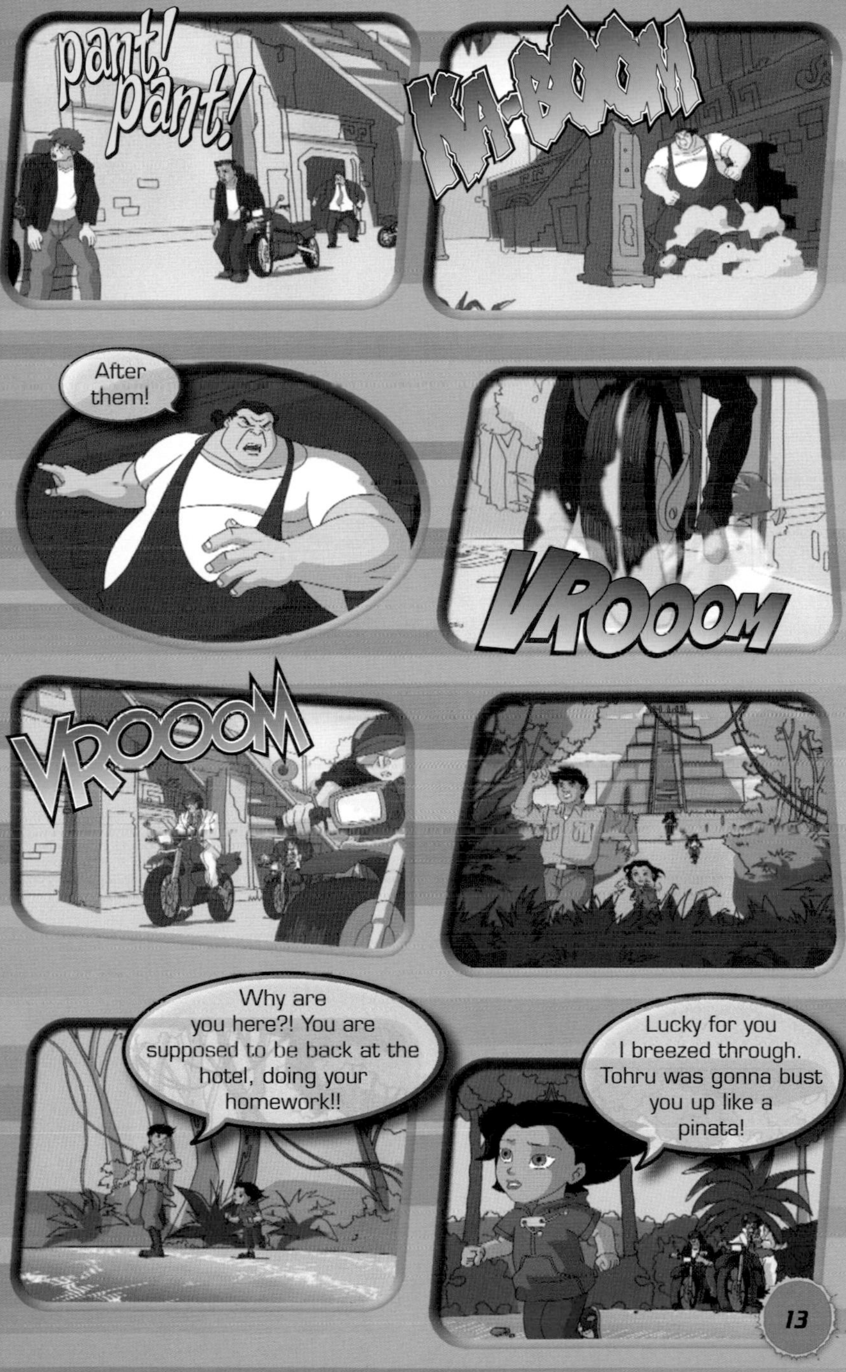
pant! pant!
KA-BOOM
After them!
VROOOM
VROOOM
Why are you here?! You are supposed to be back at the hotel, doing your homework!!
Lucky for you I breezed through. Tohru was gonna bust you up like a pinata!

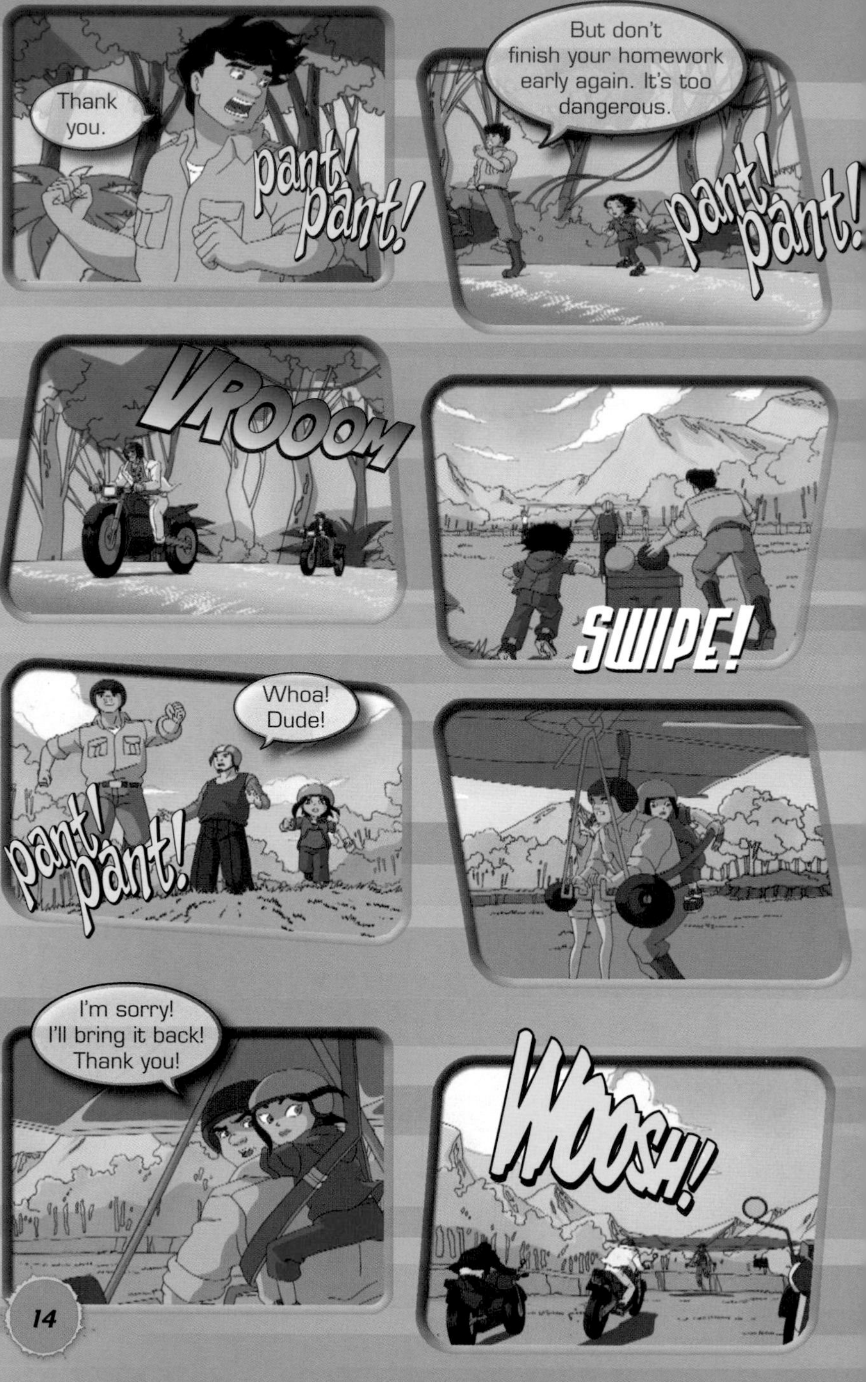
Thank you.
pant! pant!
But don't finish your homework early again. It's too dangerous.
pant! pant!
VROOOM
SWIPE!
Whoa! Dude!
pant! pant!
I'm sorry! I'll bring it back! Thank you!
WOOSH!

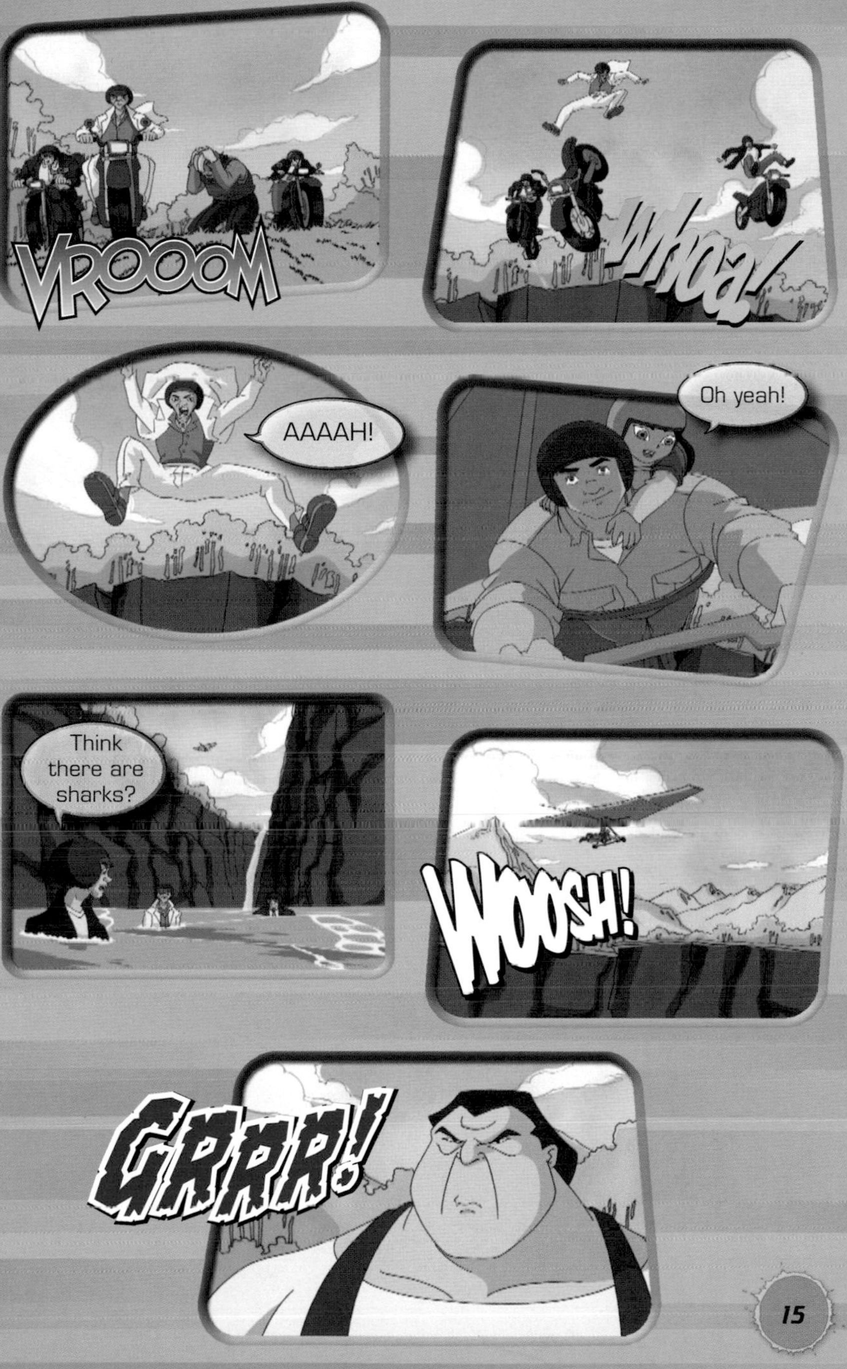
VROOOM
Whoa!
AAAAH!
Oh yeah!
Think there are sharks?
WOOSH!
GRRR!

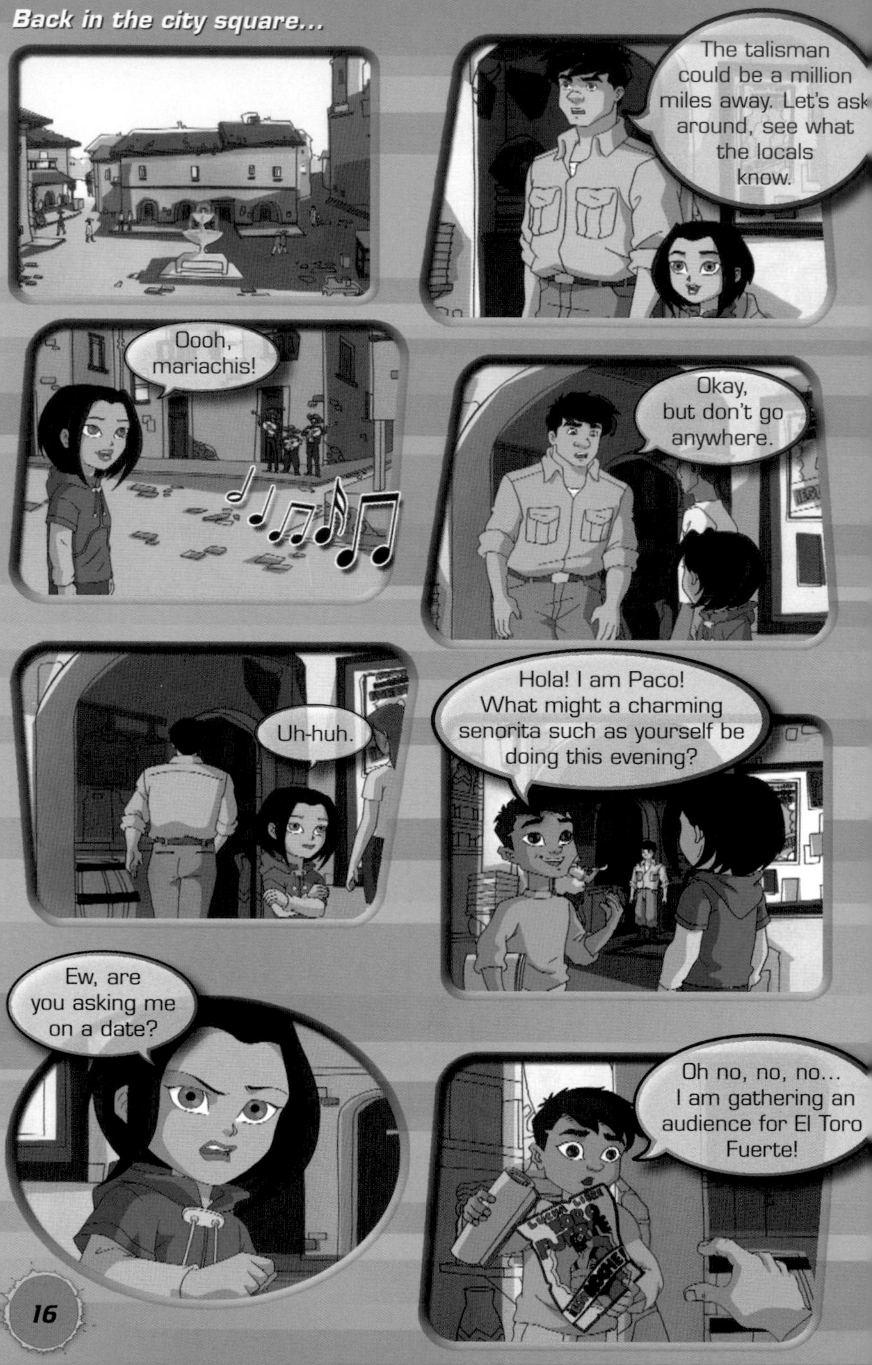
Back in the city square...
The talisman could be a million miles away. Let's ask around, see what the locals know.
Oooh, mariachis!
Okay, but don't go anywhere.
Uh-huh.
Hola! I am Paco! What might a charming senorita such as yourself be doing this evening?
Ew, are you asking me on a date?
Oh no, no, no... I am gathering an audience for El Toro Fuerte!

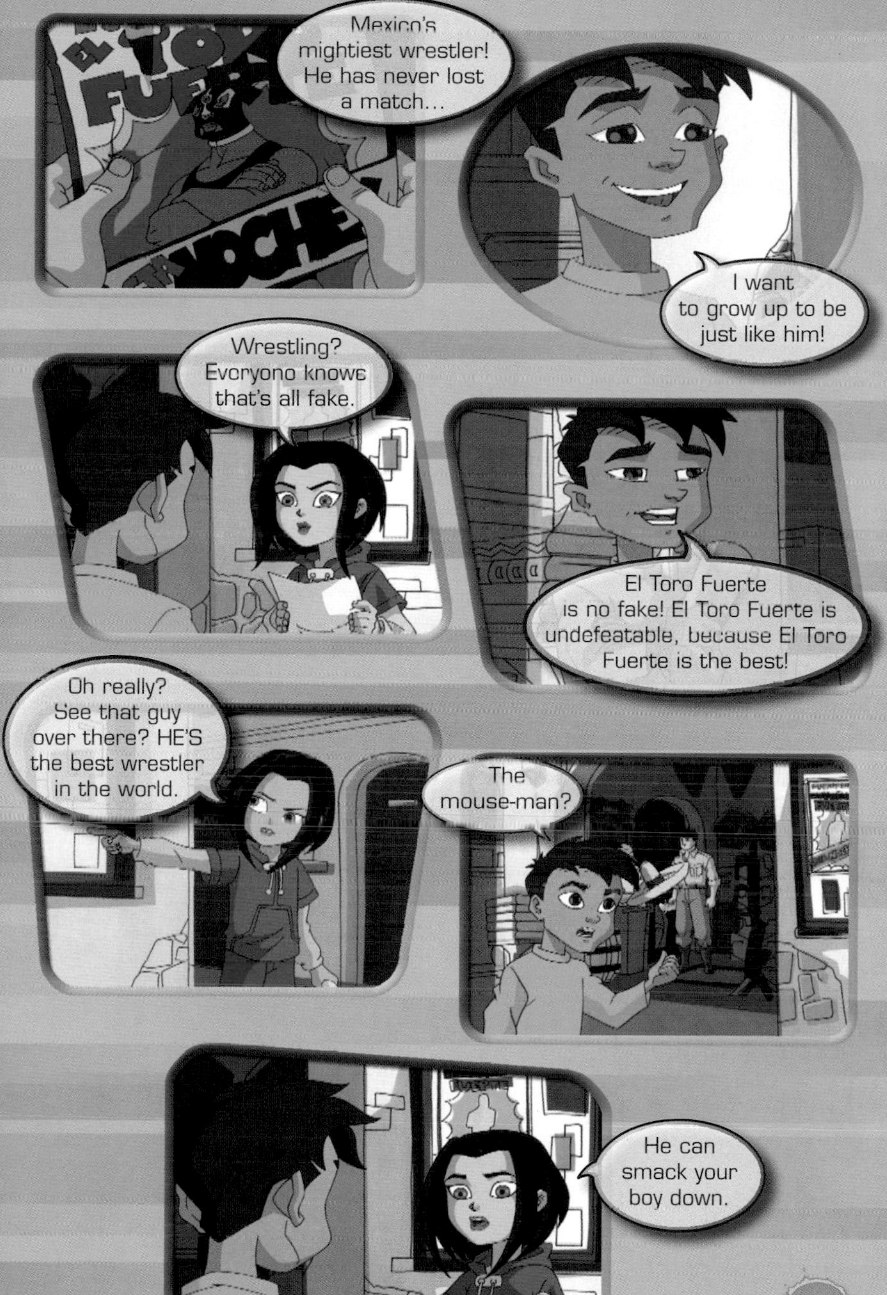
EL TORO FUERTE
Mexico's mightiest wrestler! He has never lost a match...
I want to grow up to be just like him!
Wrestling? Everyone knows that's all fake.
El Toro Fuerte is no fake! El Toro Fuerte is undefeatable, because El Toro Fuerte is the best!
Oh really? See that guy over there? HE'S the best wrestler in the world.
The mouse-man?
He can smack your boy down.

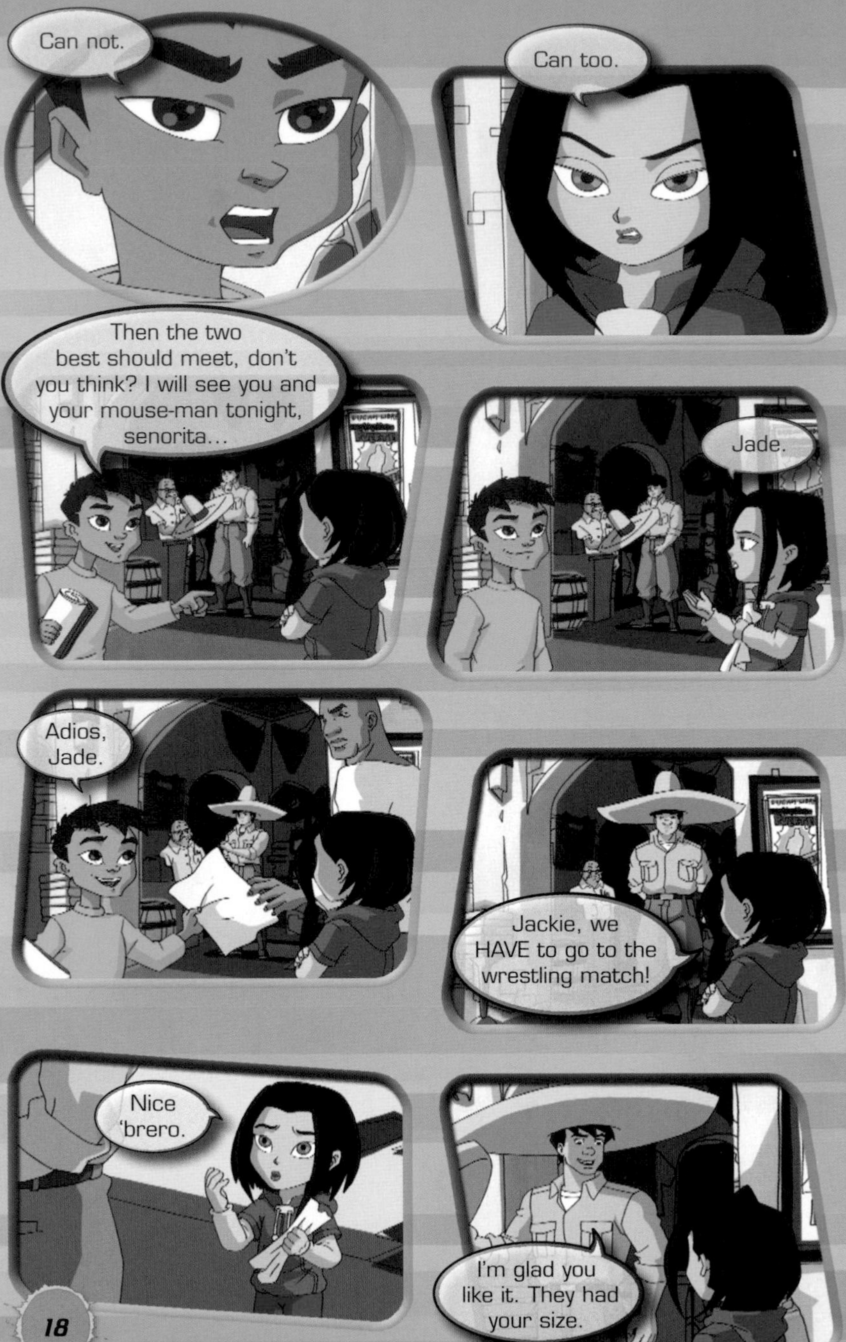
Can not.
Can too.
Then the two best should meet, don't you think? I will see you and your mouse-man tonight, senorita...
Jade.
Adios, Jade.
Jackie, we HAVE to go to the wrestling match!
Nice 'brero.
I'm glad you like it. They had your size.

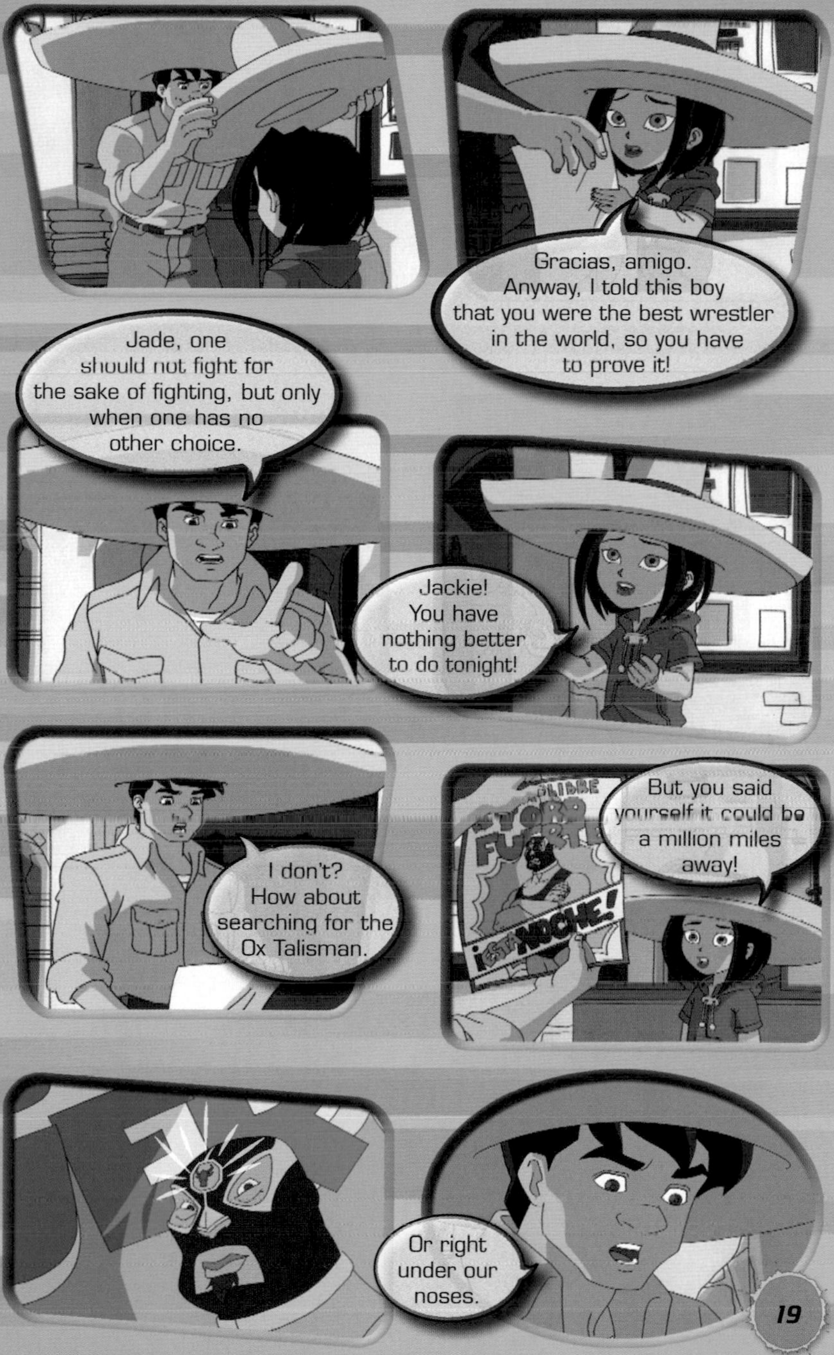
Gracias, amigo. Anyway, I told this boy that you were the best wrestler in the world, so you have to prove it!
Jade, one should not fight for the sake of fighting, but only when one has no other choice.
Jackie! You have nothing better to do tonight!
I don't? How about searching for the Ox Talisman.
¡ESTA NOCHE!
But you said yourself it could be a million miles away!
Or right under our noses.

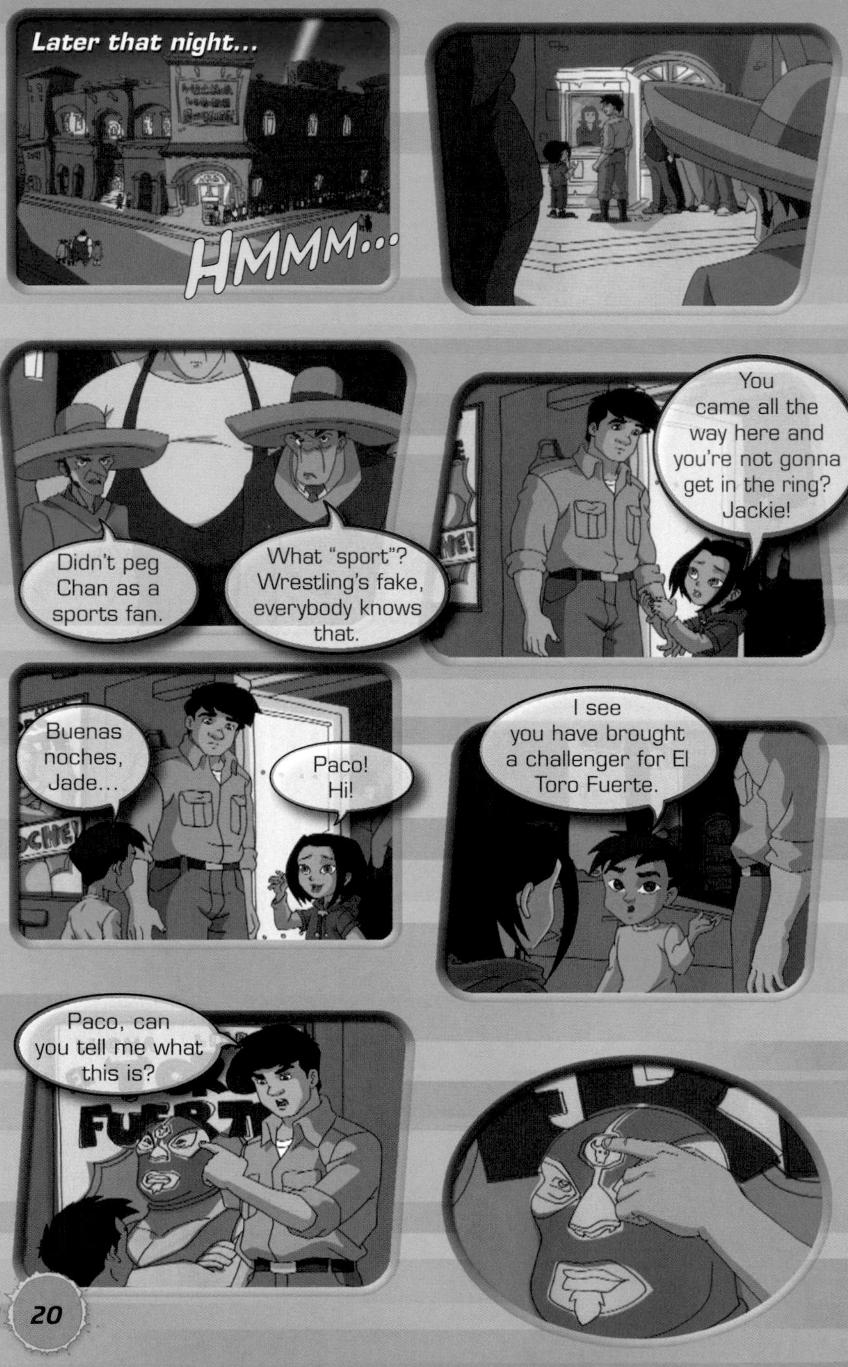
Later that night...
HMMM...
Didn't peg Chan as a sports fan.
What "sport"? Wrestling's fake, everybody knows that.
You came all the way here and you're not gonna get in the ring? Jackie!
Buenas noches, Jade...
Paco! Hi!
I see you have brought a challenger for El Toro Fuerte.
Paco, can you tell me what this is?
FUERT

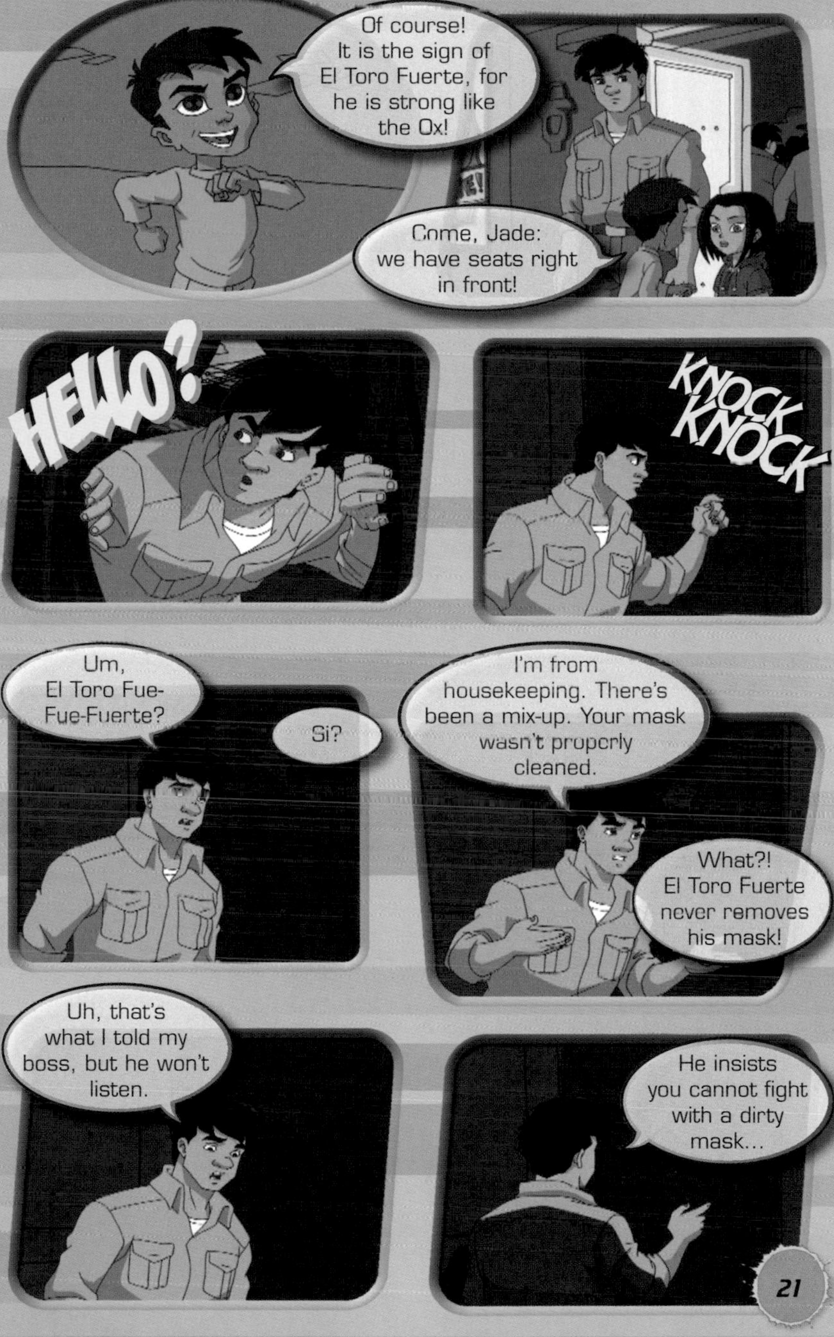

Of course! It is the sign of El Toro Fuerte, for he is strong like the Ox!
Come, Jade: we have seats right in front!
HELLO?
KNOCK KNOCK
Um, El Toro Fue-Fue-Fuerte?
Si?
I'm from housekeeping. There's been a mix-up. Your mask wasn't properly cleaned.
What?! El Toro Fuerte never removes his mask!
Uh, that's what I told my boss, but he won't listen.
He insists you cannot fight with a dirty mask...

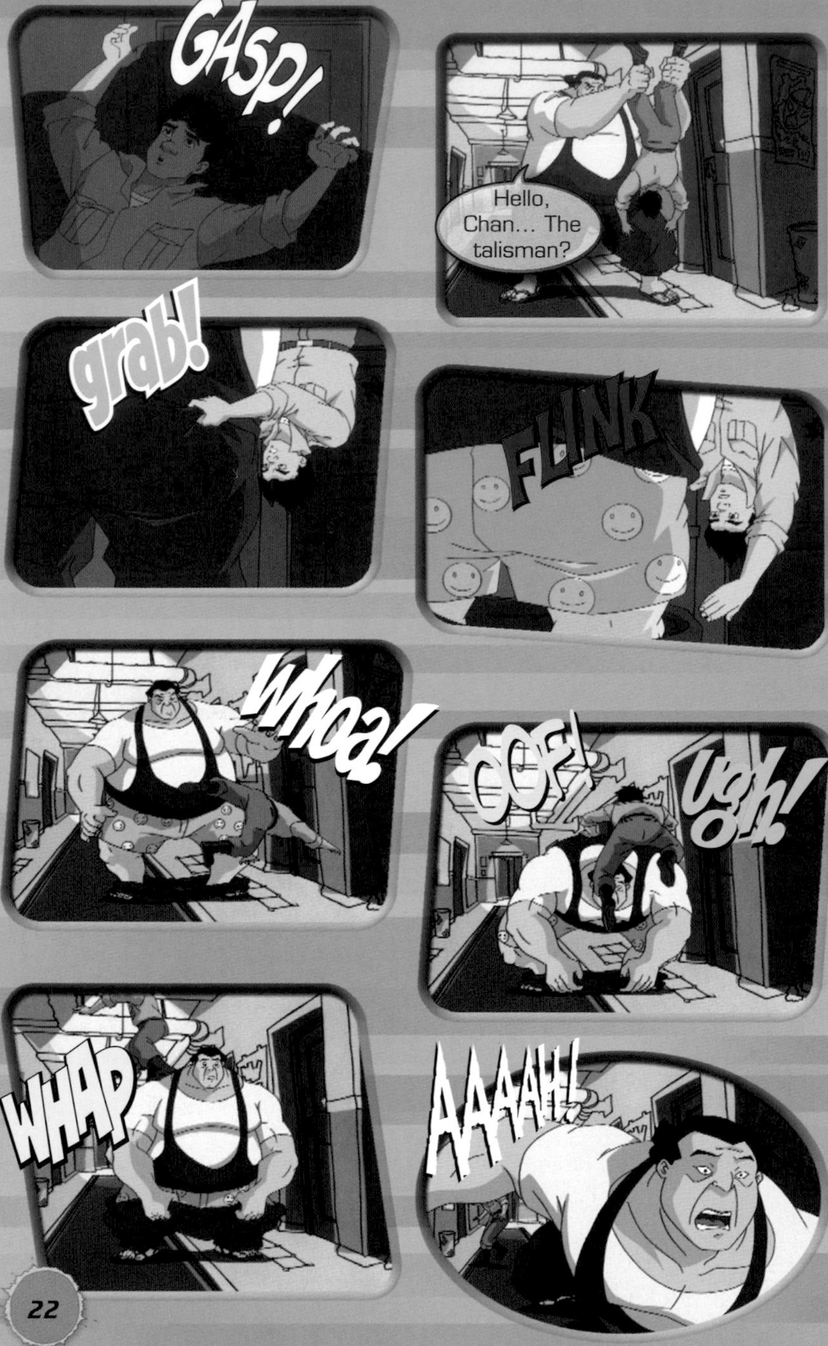
GASP!
Hello, Chan... The talisman?
grab!
FLINK
whoa!
OOF!
ugh!
WHAP
AAAAH!

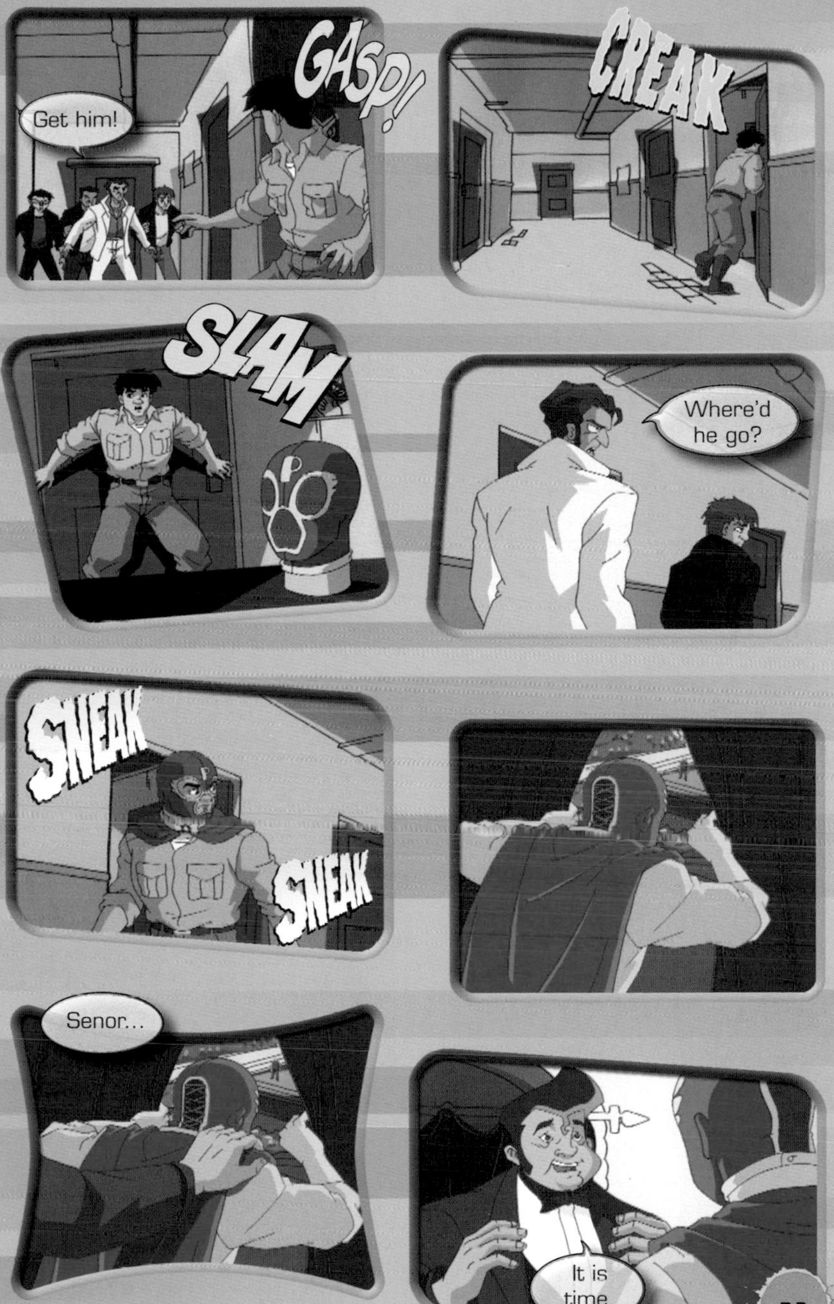
Get him!
GASP!
CREAK
SLAM
Where'd he go?
SNEAK
SNEAK
Senor...
It is time.

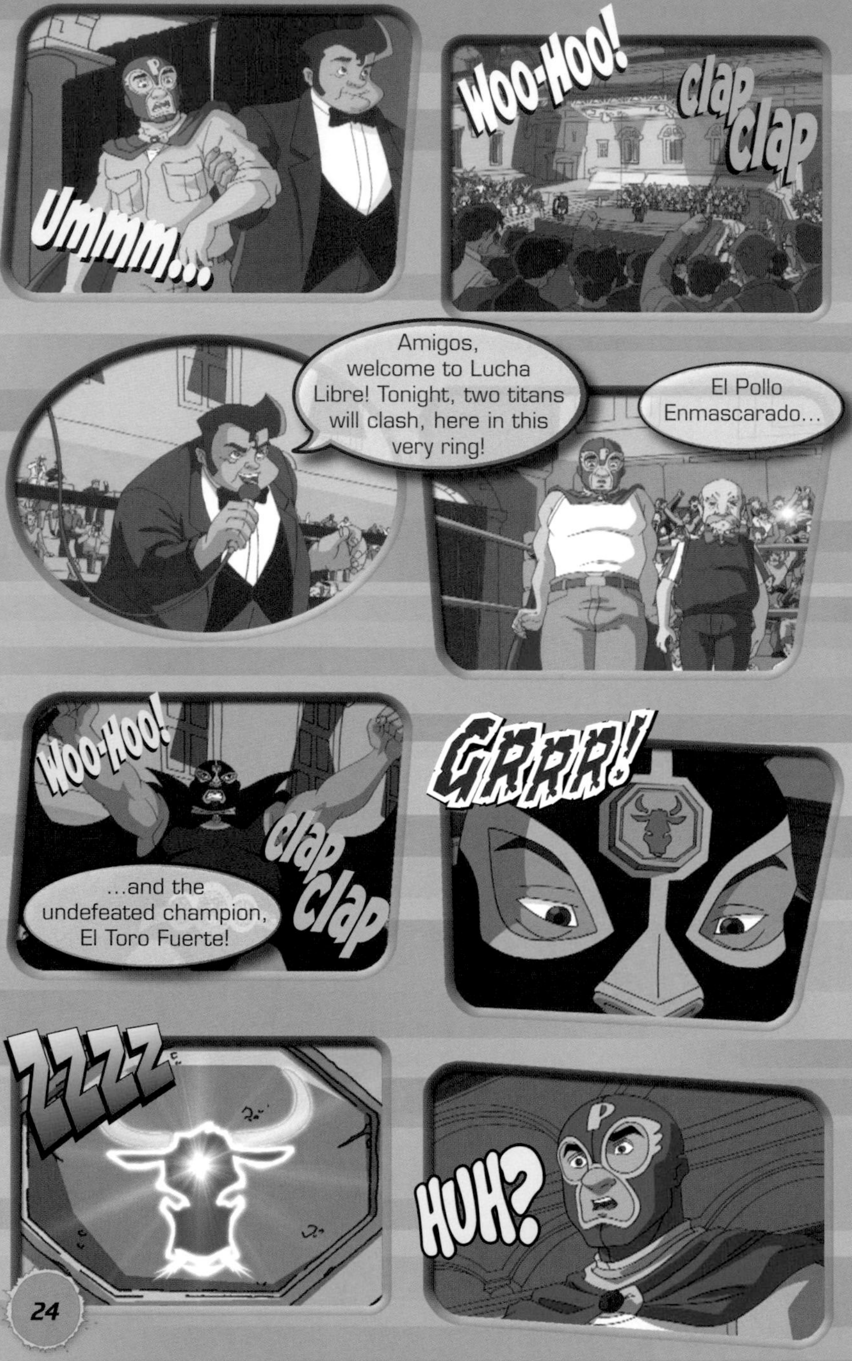
UMMM...
WOO-HOO!
clap clap
Amigos, welcome to Lucha Libre! Tonight, two titans will clash, here in this very ring!
El Pollo Enmascarado...
WOO-HOO!
clap clap
...and the undefeated champion, El Toro Fuerte!
GRRR!
ZZZZ
HUH?

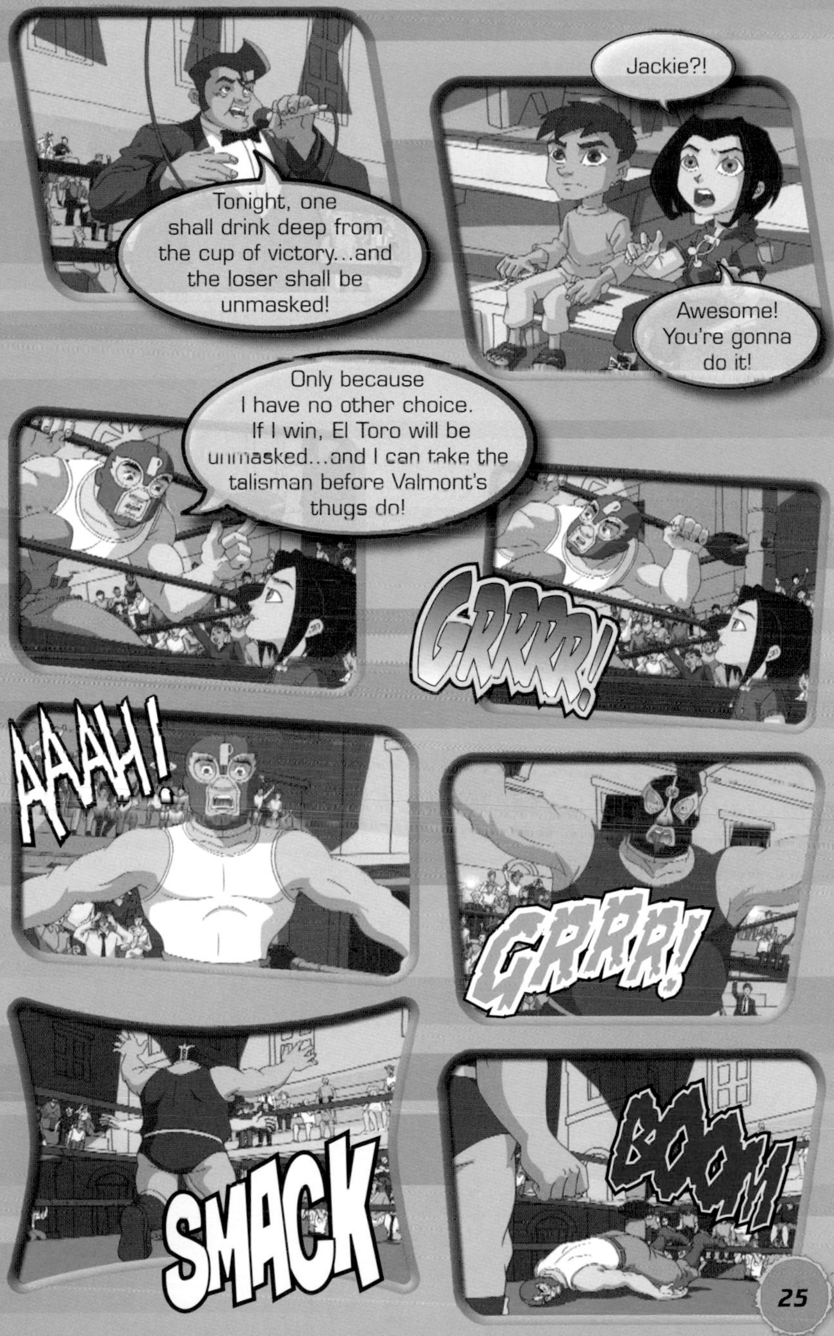

Tonight, one shall drink deep from the cup of victory...and the loser shall be unmasked!
Jackie?!
Awesome! You're gonna do it!
Only because I have no other choice. If I win, El Toro will be unmasked...and I can take the talisman before Valmont's thugs do!
GRRRR!
AAAH!
GRRR!
SMACK
BOOM

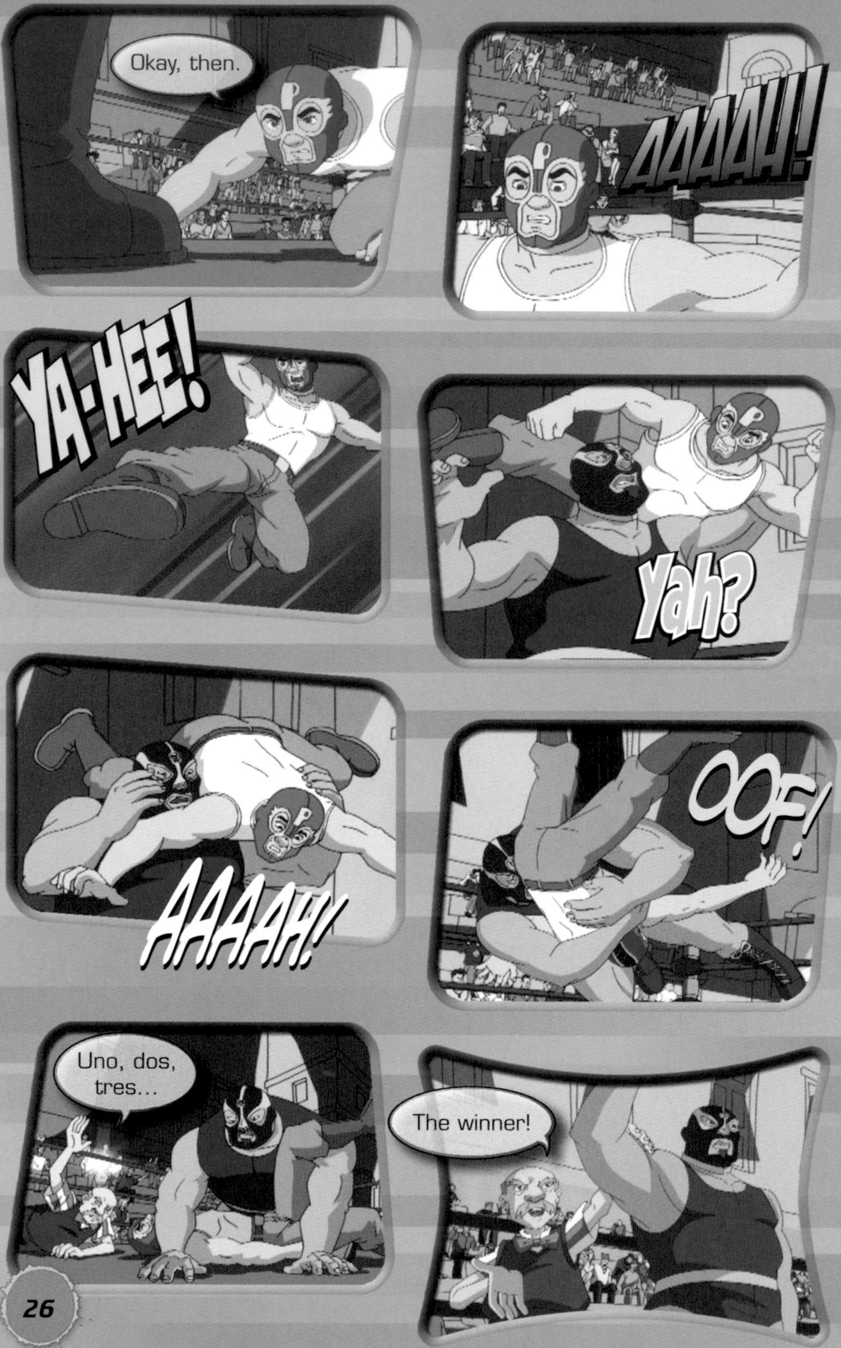
Okay, then.
AAAAH!
YA-HEE!
Yah?
AAAAH!
OOF!
Uno, dos, tres...
The winner!

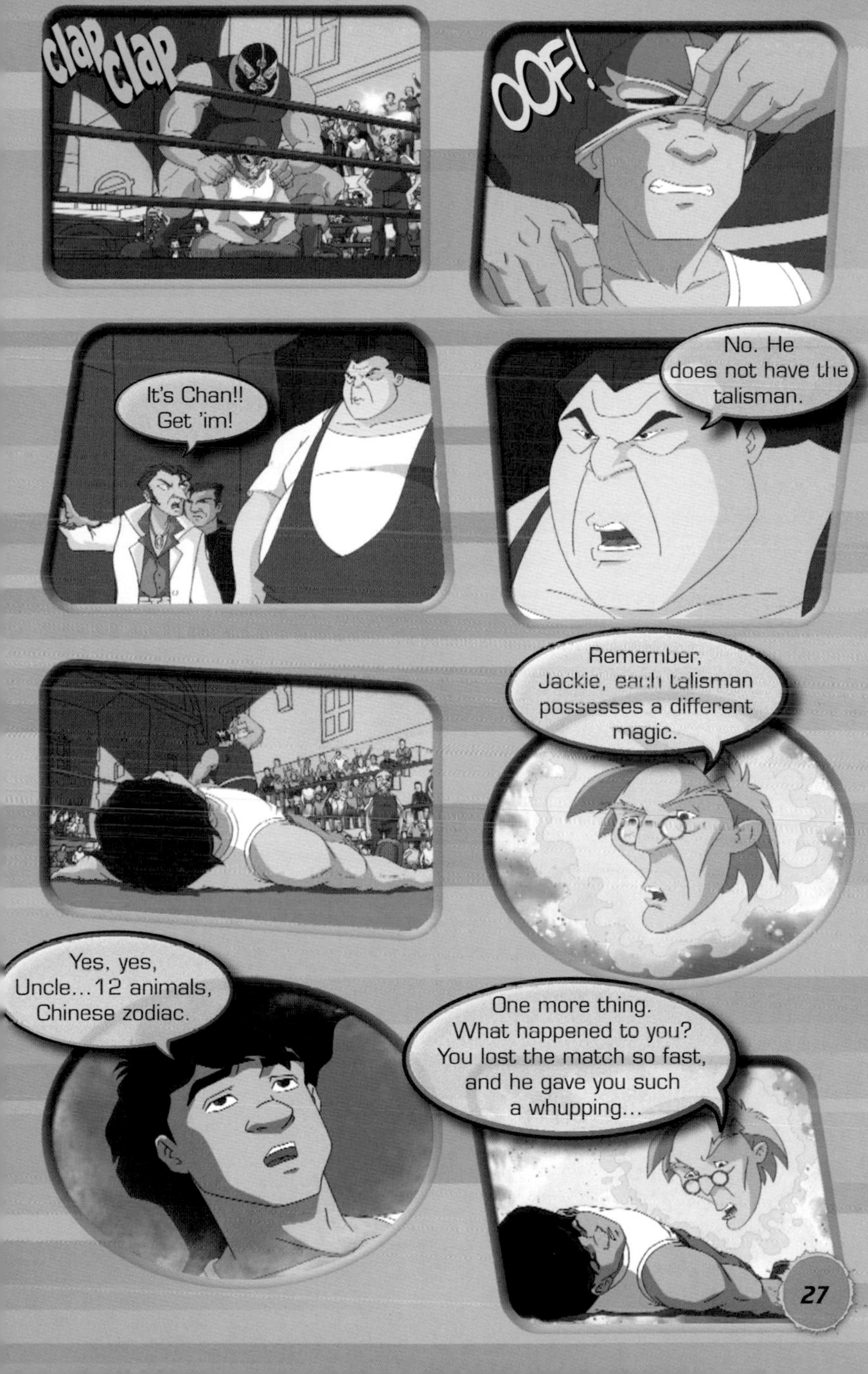
clap clap
OOF!
It's Chan!! Get 'im!
No. He does not have the talisman.
Remember, Jackie, each talisman possesses a different magic.
Yes, yes, Uncle...12 animals, Chinese zodiac.
One more thing. What happened to you? You lost the match so fast, and he gave you such a whupping...

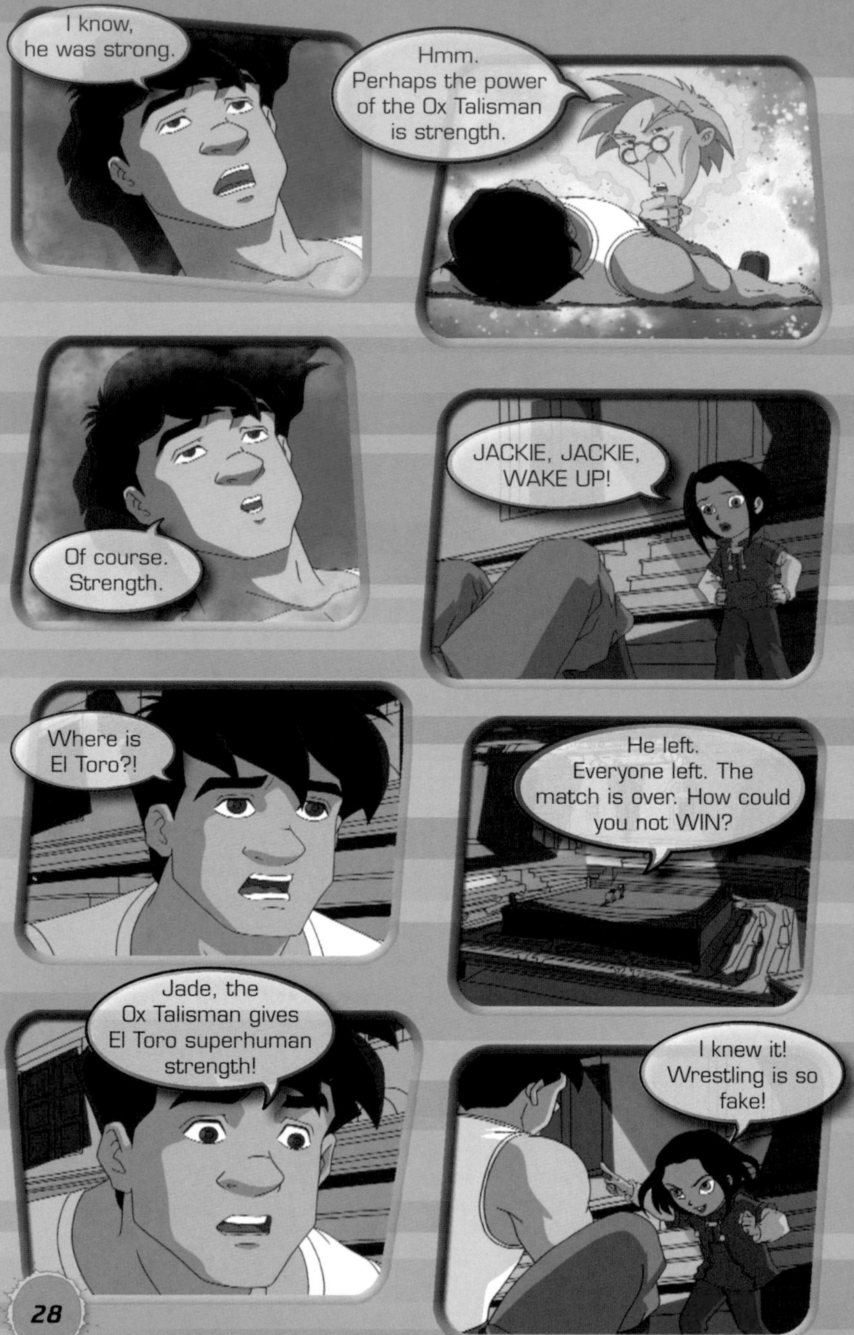
I know, he was strong.
Hmm. Perhaps the power of the Ox Talisman is strength.
Of course. Strength.
JACKIE, JACKIE, WAKE UP!
Where is El Toro?!
He left. Everyone left. The match is over. How could you not WIN?
Jade, the Ox Talisman gives El Toro superhuman strength!
I knew it! Wrestling is so fake!

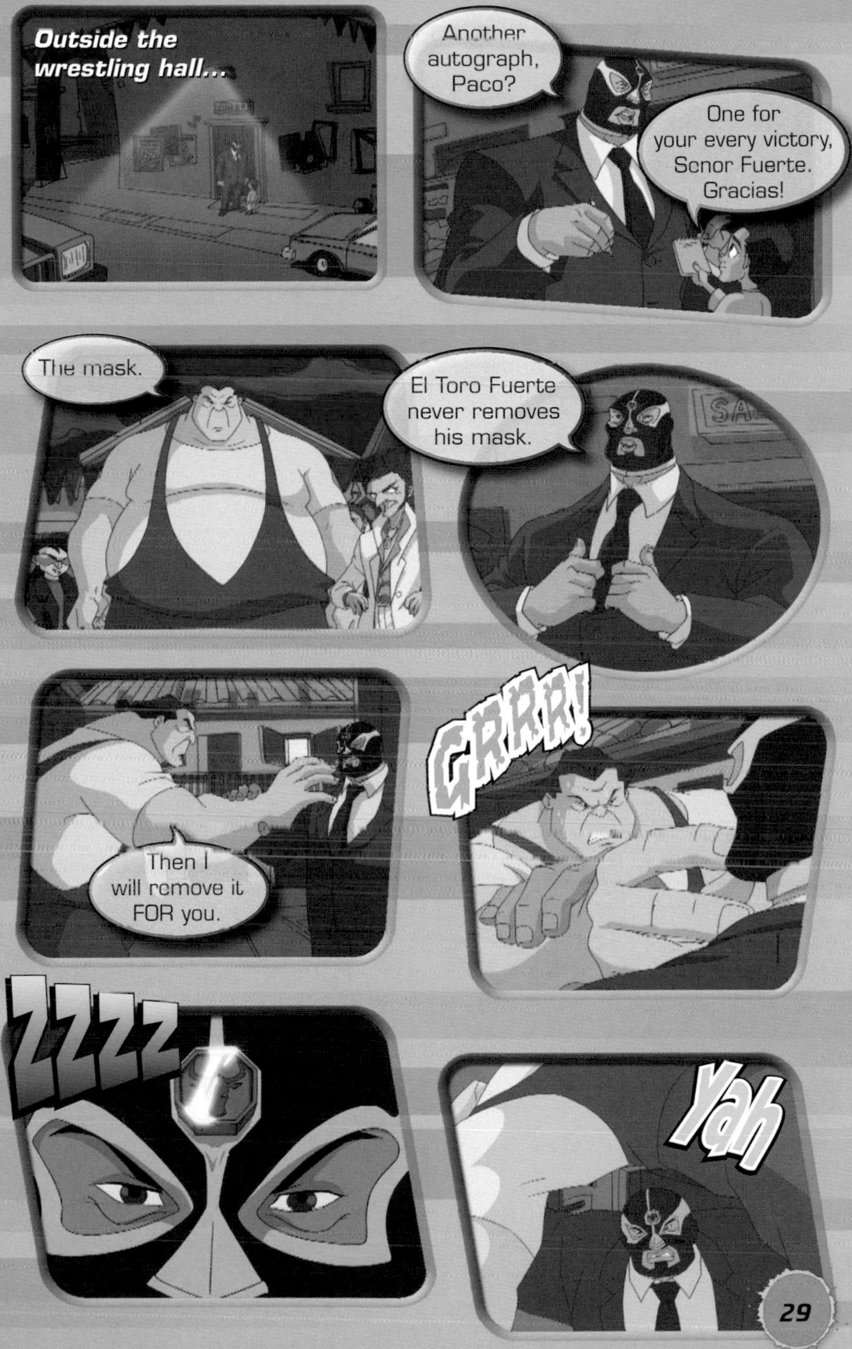

Outside the wrestling hall...
Another autograph, Paco?
One for your every victory, Scnor Fuerte. Gracias!
The mask.
El Toro Fuerte never removes his mask.
Then I will remove it FOR you.
GRRR!
ZZZZ
Yah

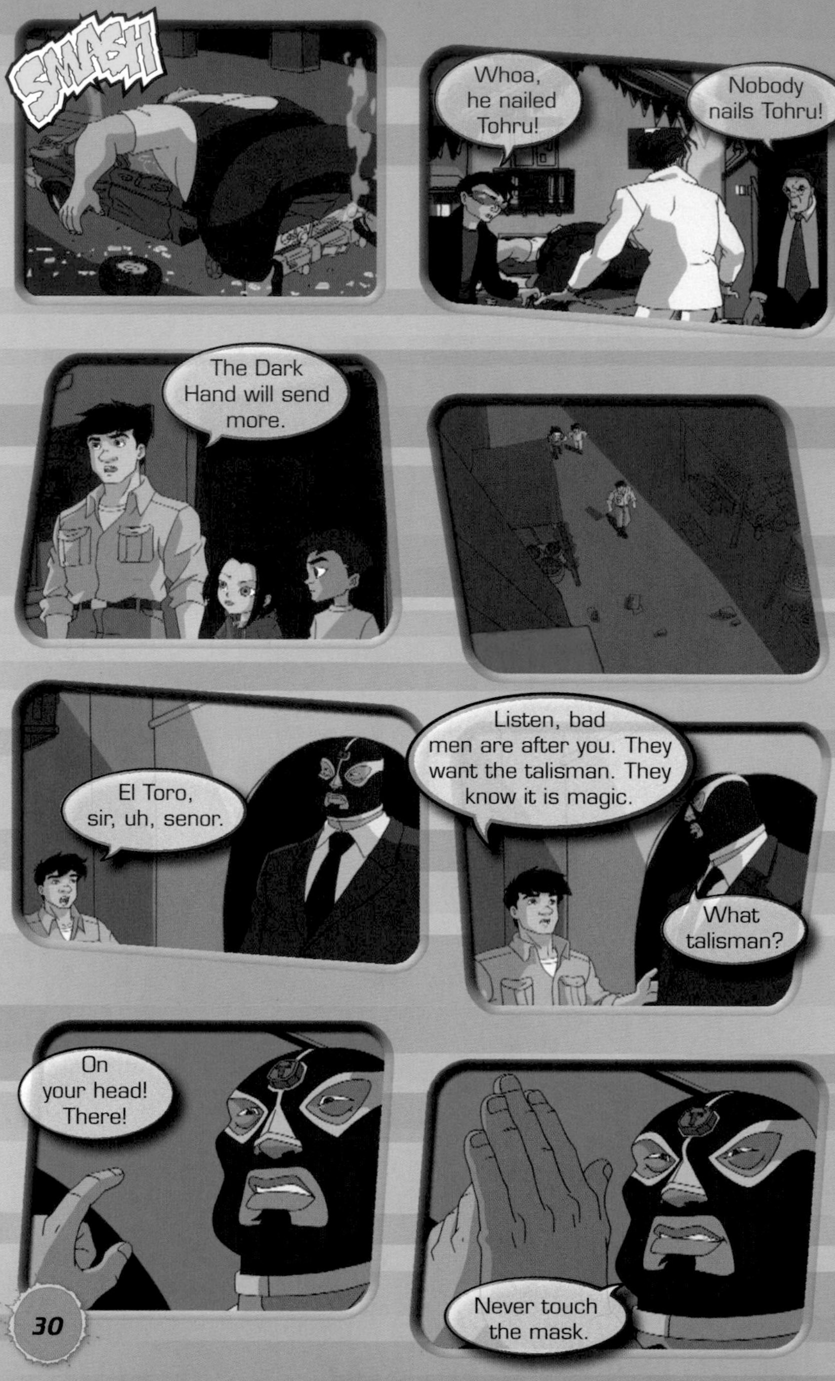
SMASH
Whoa, he nailed Tohru!
Nobody nails Tohru!
The Dark Hand will send more.
El Toro, sir, uh, senor.
Listen, bad men are after you. They want the talisman. They know it is magic.
What talisman?
On your head! There!
Never touch the mask.

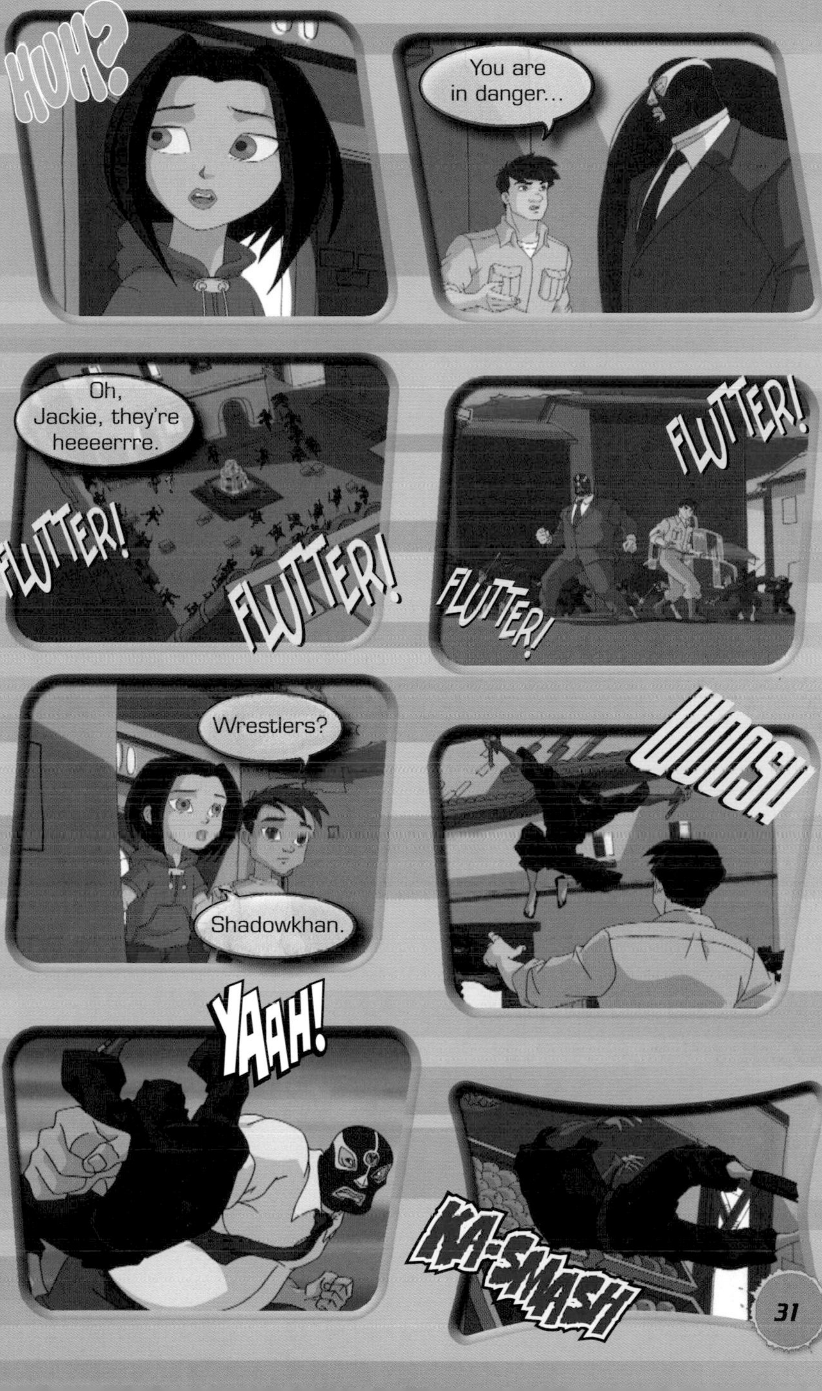
HUH?
You are in danger...
Oh, Jackie, they're heeeerrre.
FLUTTER!
FLUTTER!
FLUTTER!
FLUTTER!
Wrestlers?
Shadowkhan.
WOOSH
YAAH!
KA-SMASH

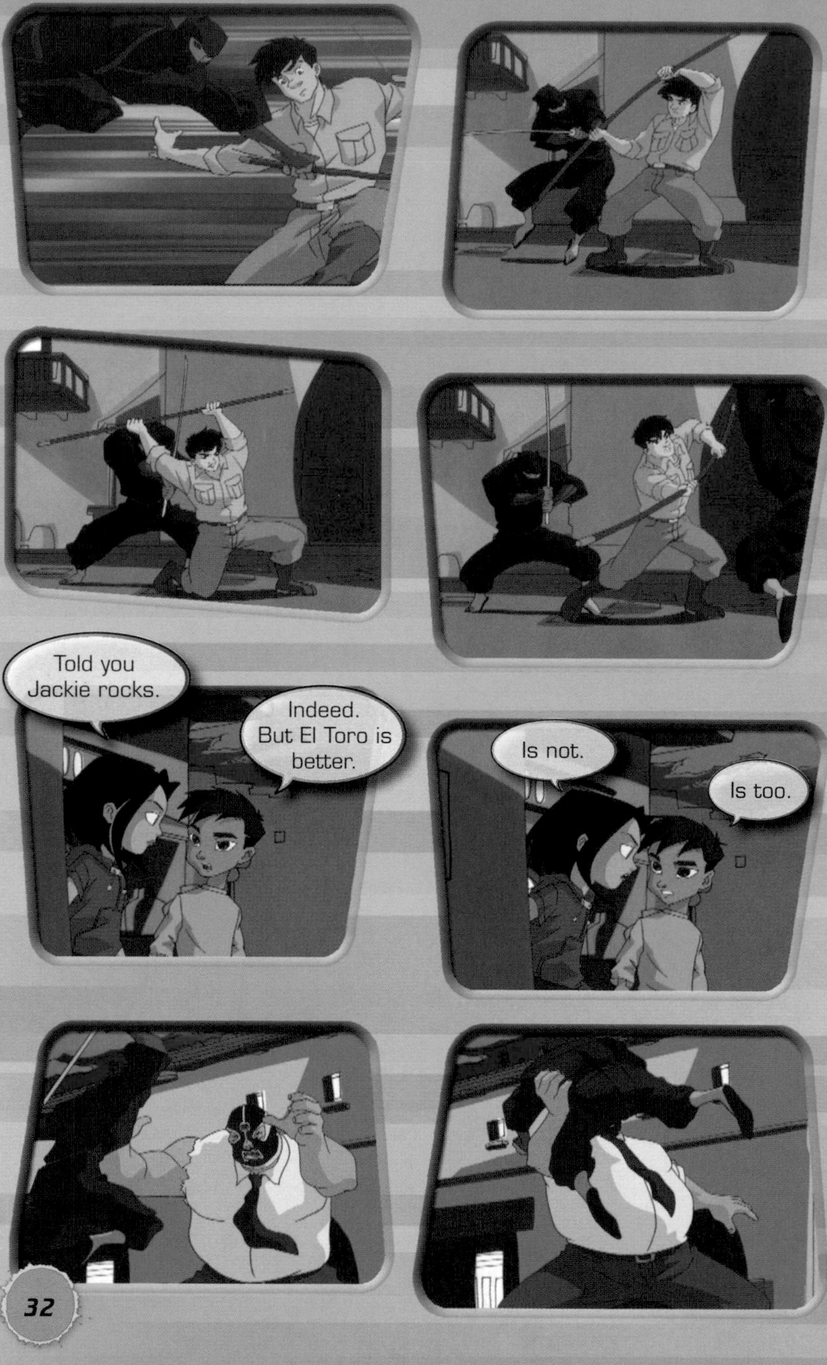
Told you Jackie rocks.
Indeed. But El Toro is better.
Is not.
Is too.

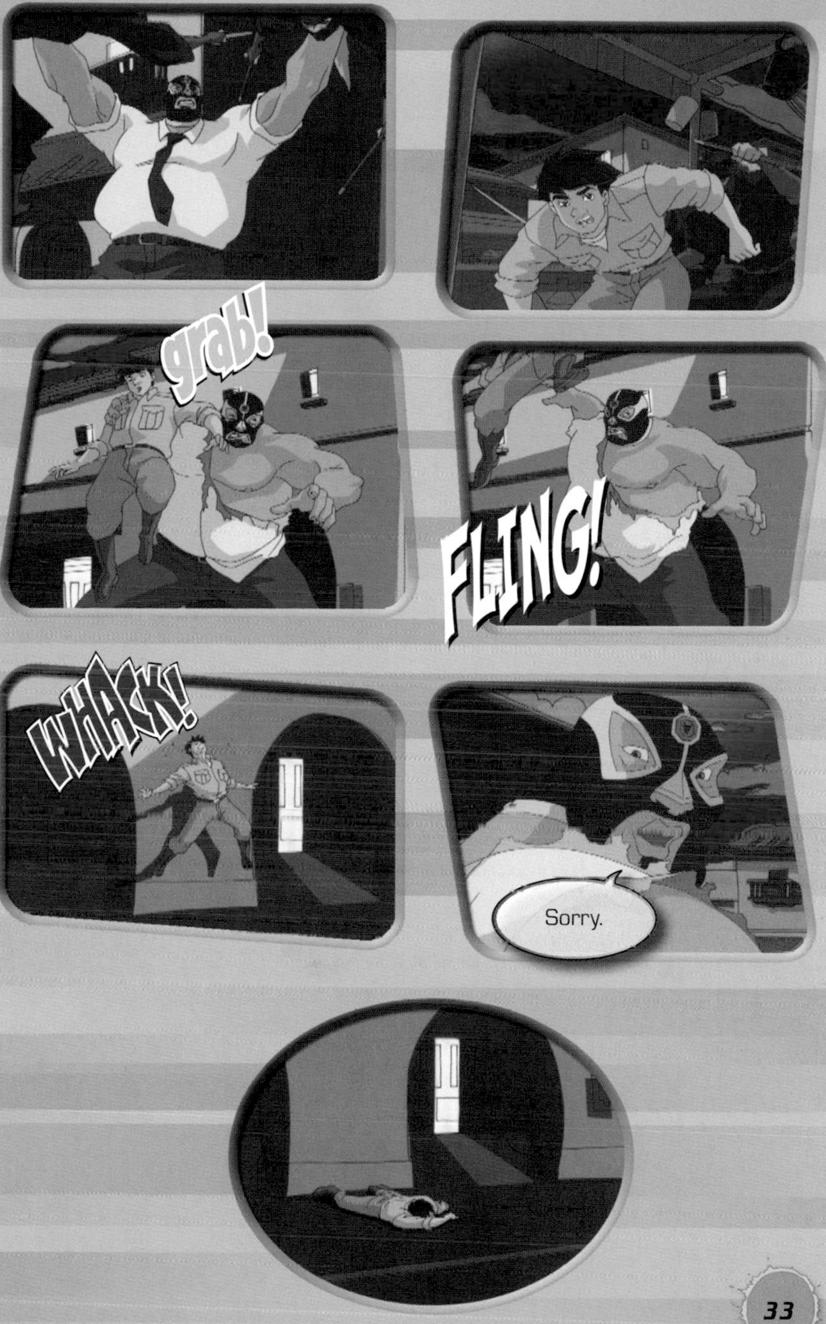
grab!
FLING!
WHACK!
Sorry.

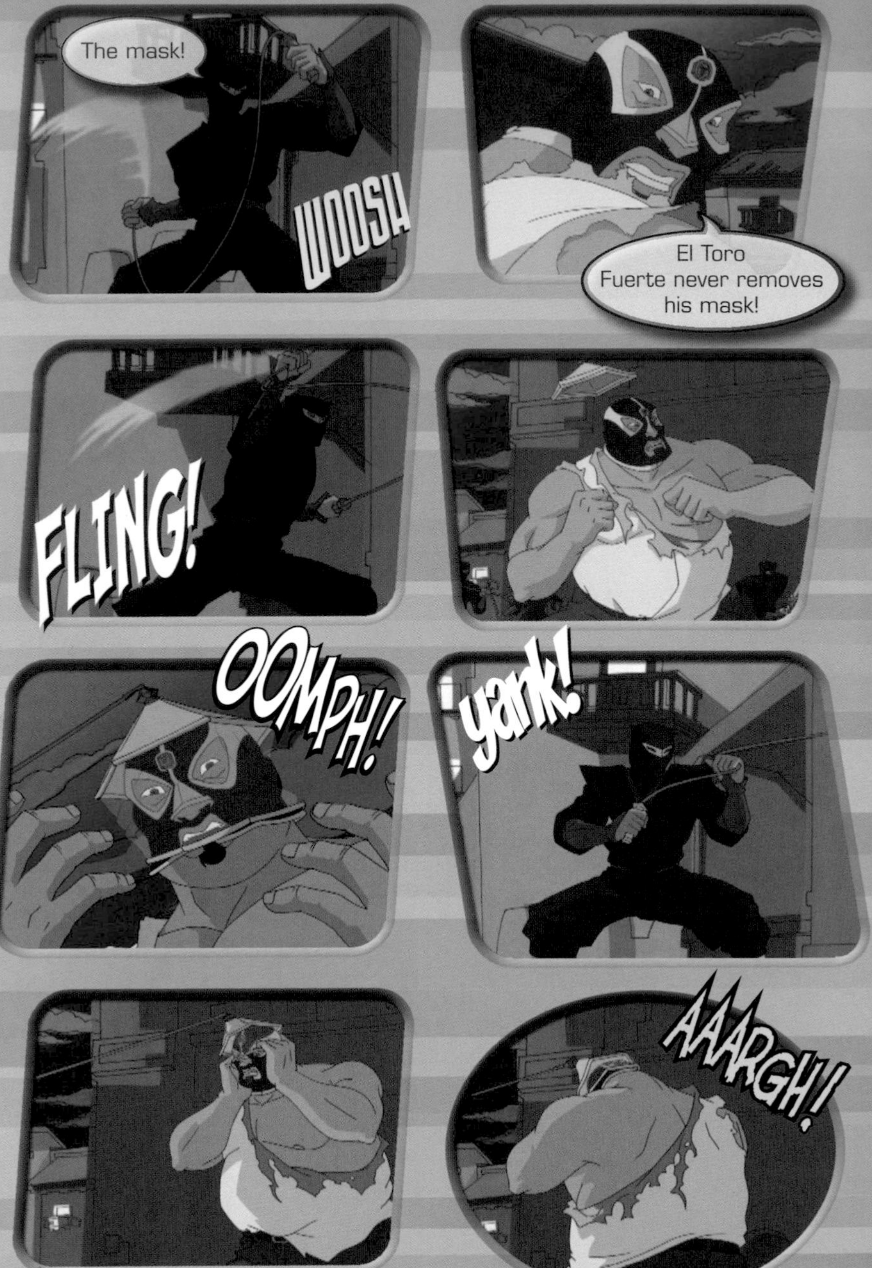
The mask!
WOOSH
El Toro Fuerte never removes his mask!
FLING!
OOMPH!
yank!
AAARGH!

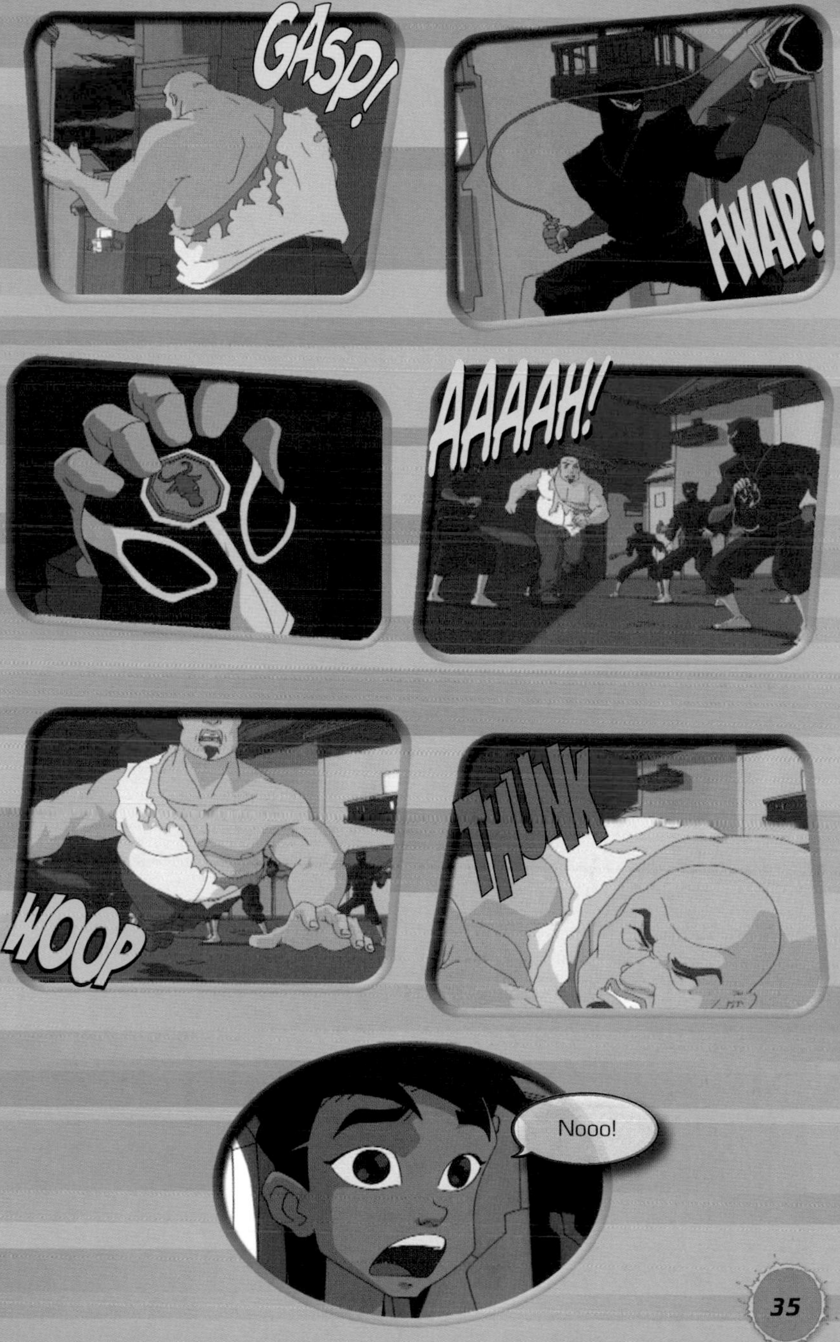
GASP!
FWAP!
AAAAH!
WOOP
THUNK
Nooo!

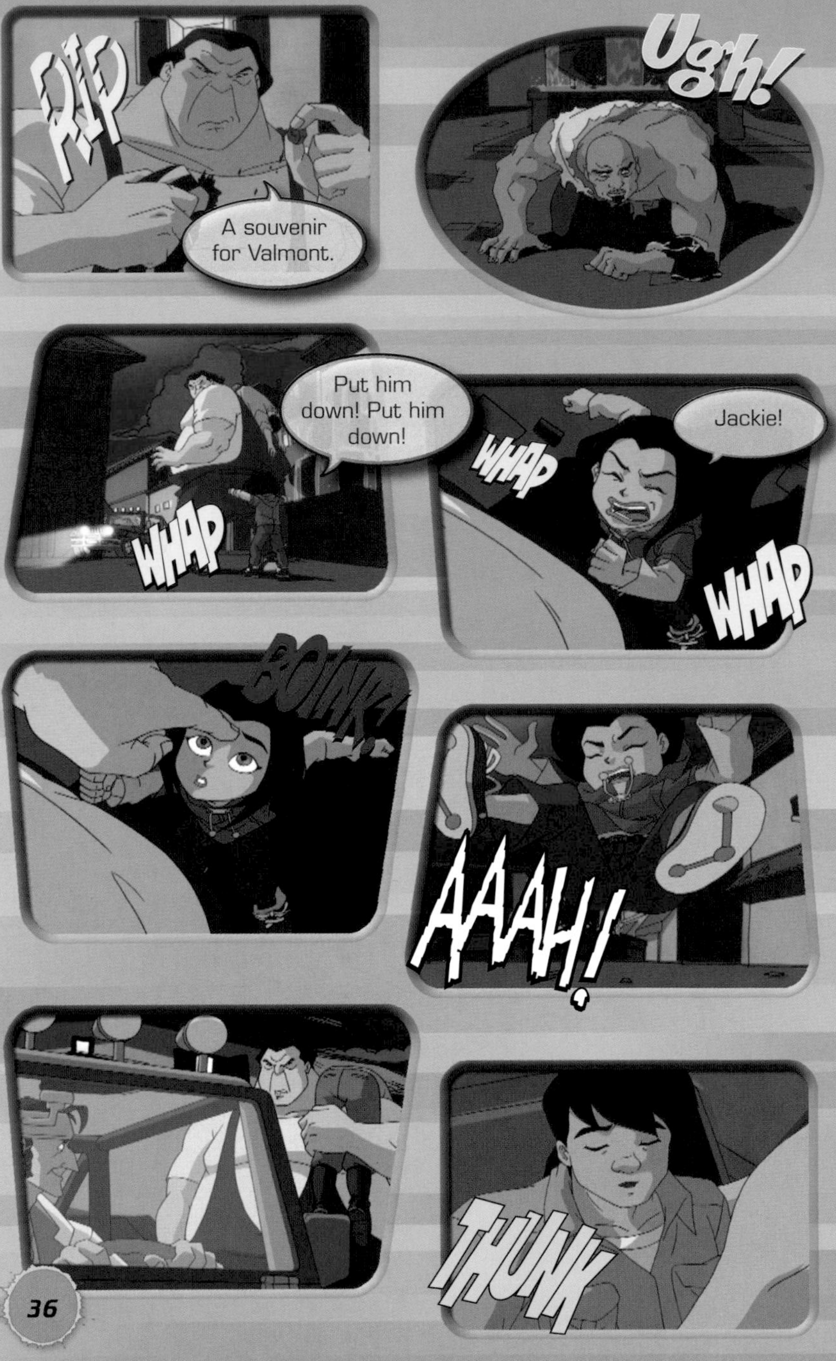
RIP
A souvenir for Valmont.
Ugh!
Put him down! Put him down!
WHAP
Jackie!
WHAP
WHAP
BOINK!
AAAH!
THUNK

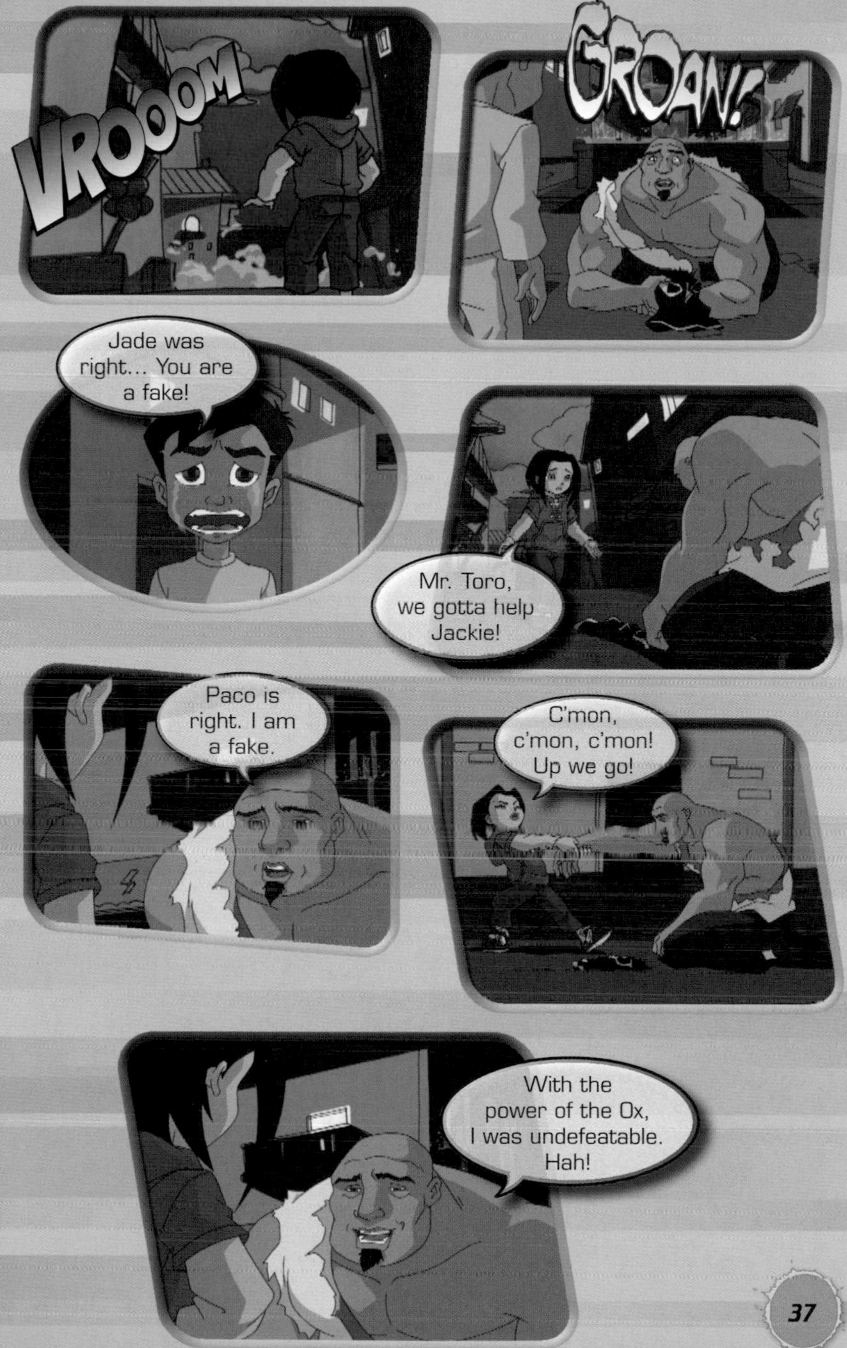
VROOOM
GROAN!
Jade was right... You are a fake!
Mr. Toro, we gotta help Jackie!
Paco is right. I am a fake.
C'mon, c'mon, c'mon! Up we go!
With the power of the Ox, I was undefeatable. Hah!

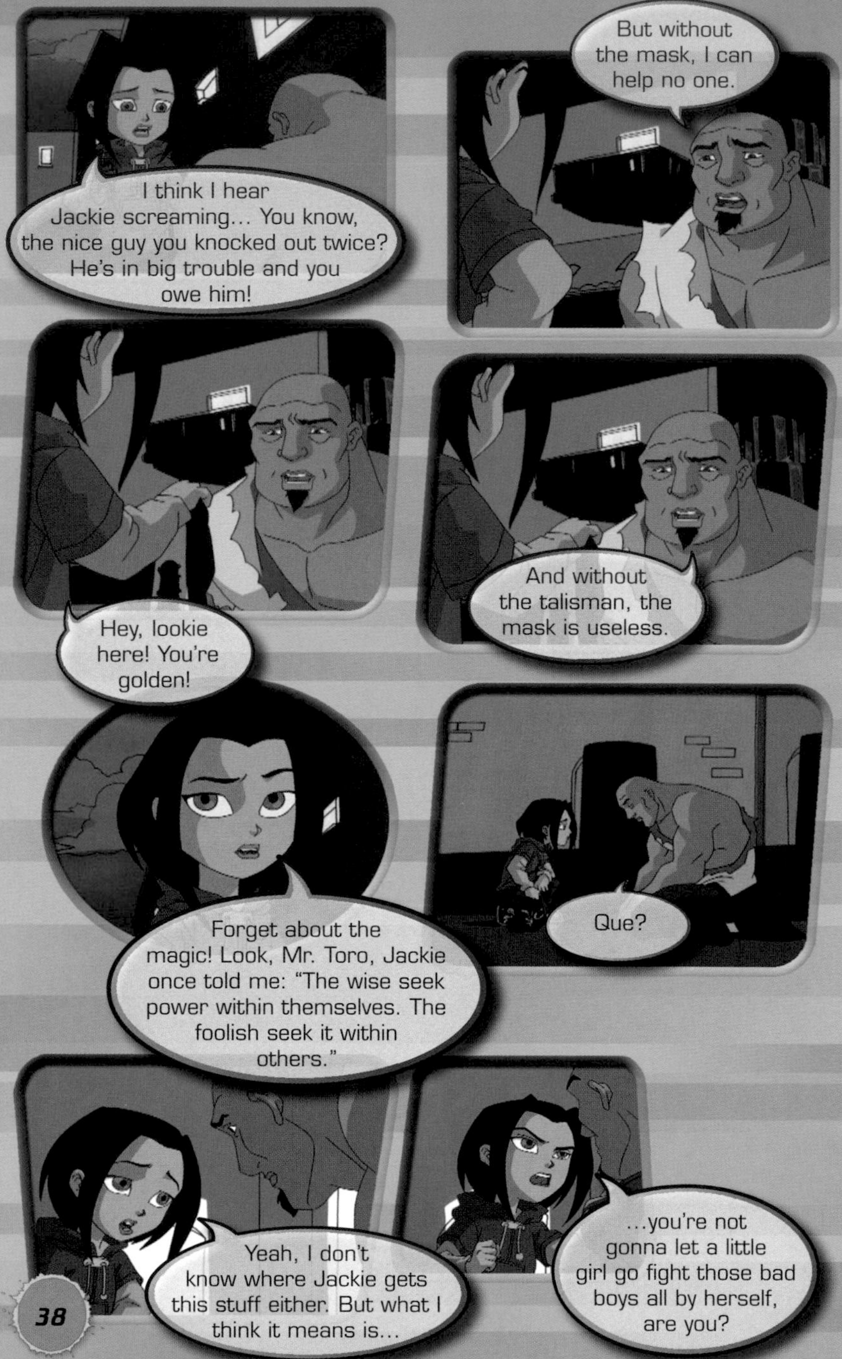
I think I hear Jackie screaming... You know, the nice guy you knocked out twice? He's in big trouble and you owe him!
But without the mask, I can help no one.
Hey, lookie here! You're golden!
And without the talisman, the mask is useless.
Forget about the magic! Look, Mr. Toro, Jackie once told me: "The wise seek power within themselves. The foolish seek it within others."
Que?
Yeah, I don't know where Jackie gets this stuff either. But what I think it means is...
...you're not gonna let a little girl go fight those bad boys all by herself, are you?

At an airport nearby...

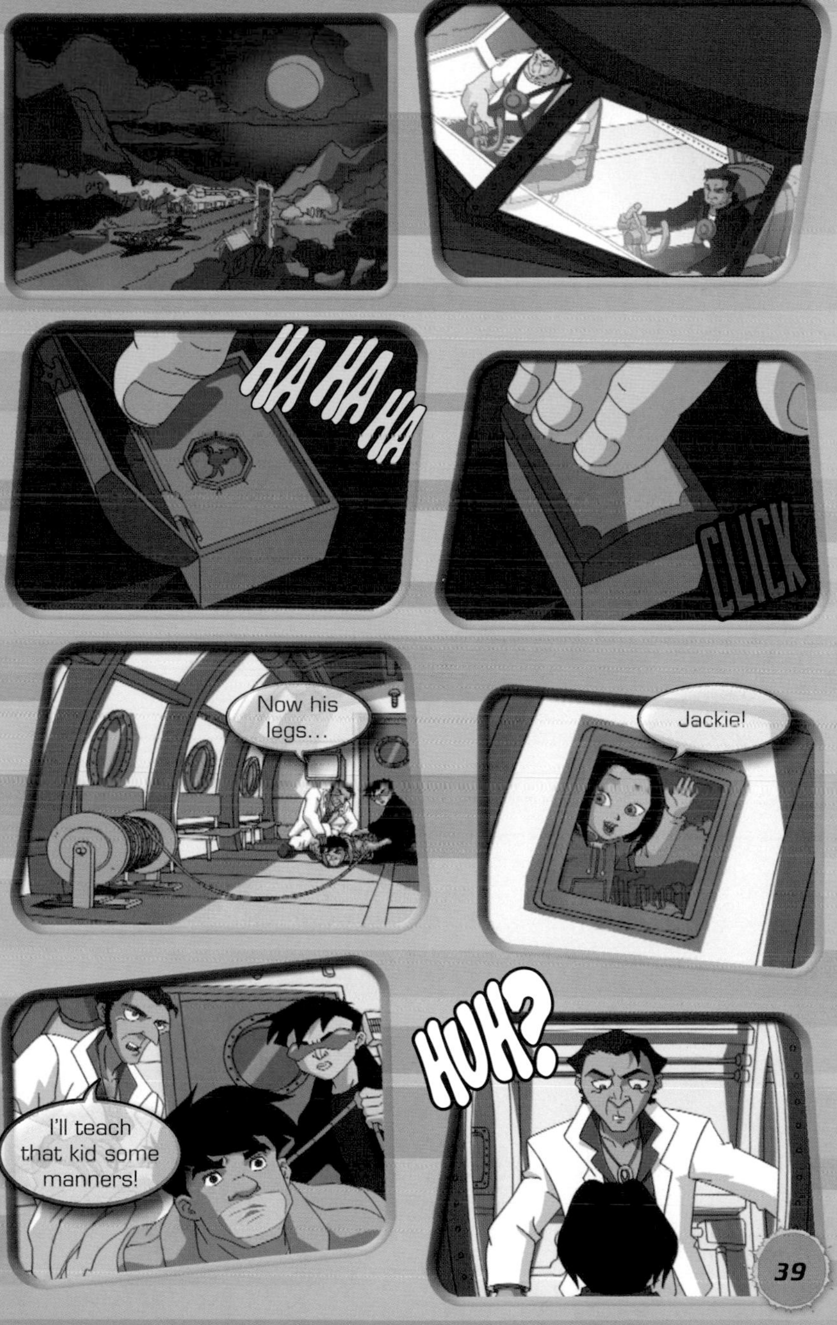
HA HA HA HA
CLICK
Now his legs...
Jackie!
I'll teach that kid some manners!
HUH?

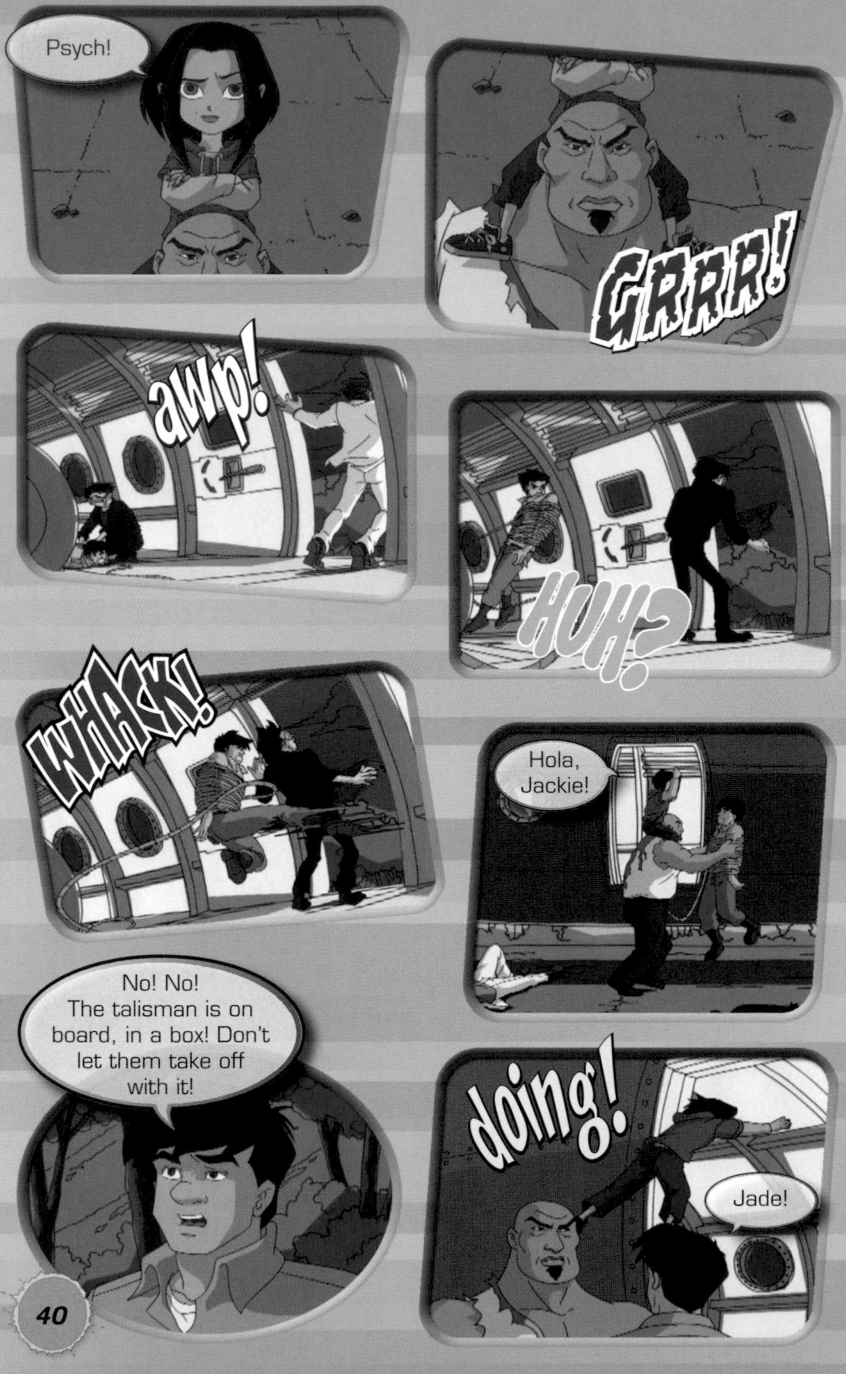
Psych!
GRRR!
awp!
HUH?
WHACK!
Hola, Jackie!
No! No! The talisman is on board, in a box! Don't let them take off with it!
doing!
Jade!

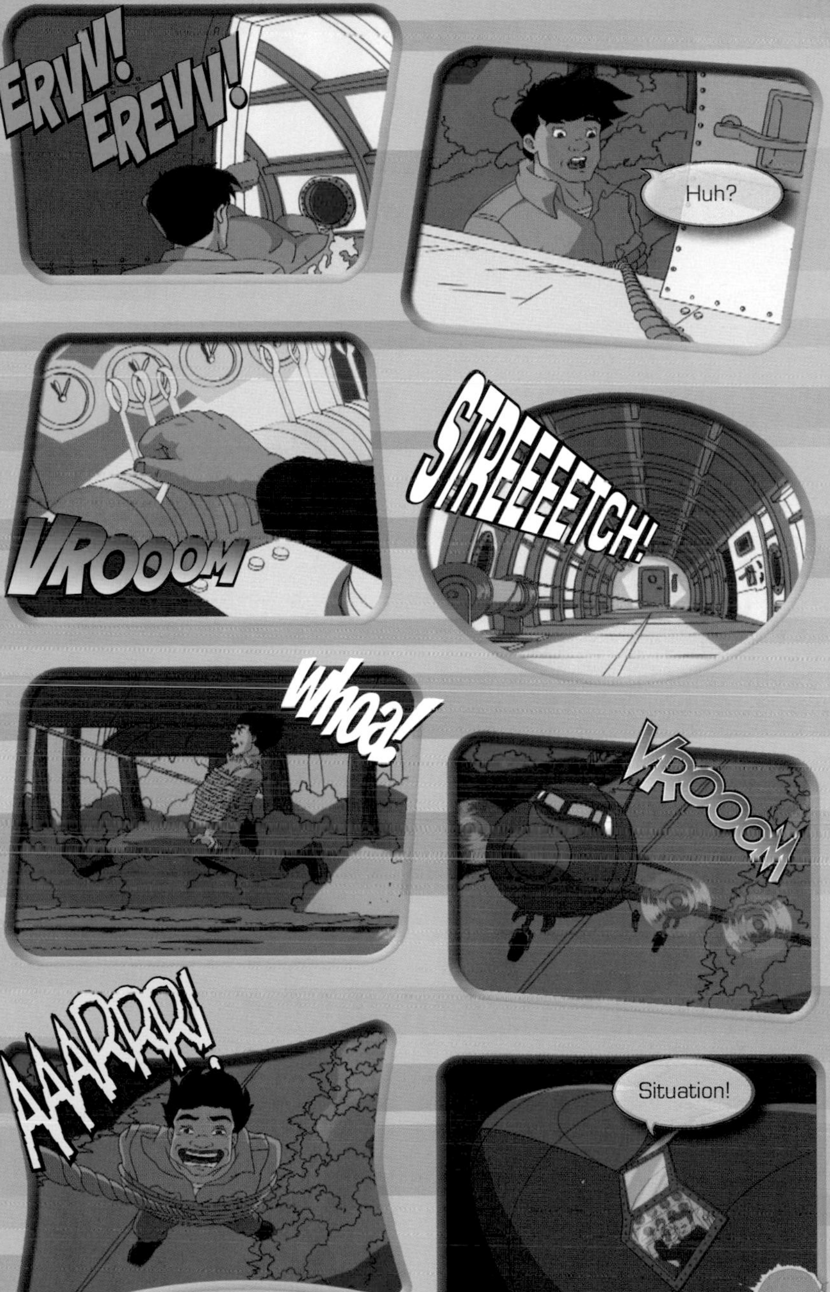
ERVV! EREVV!
Huh?
VROOOM
STREEEEETCH!
whoa!
VROOOM
AAARRR!
Situation!

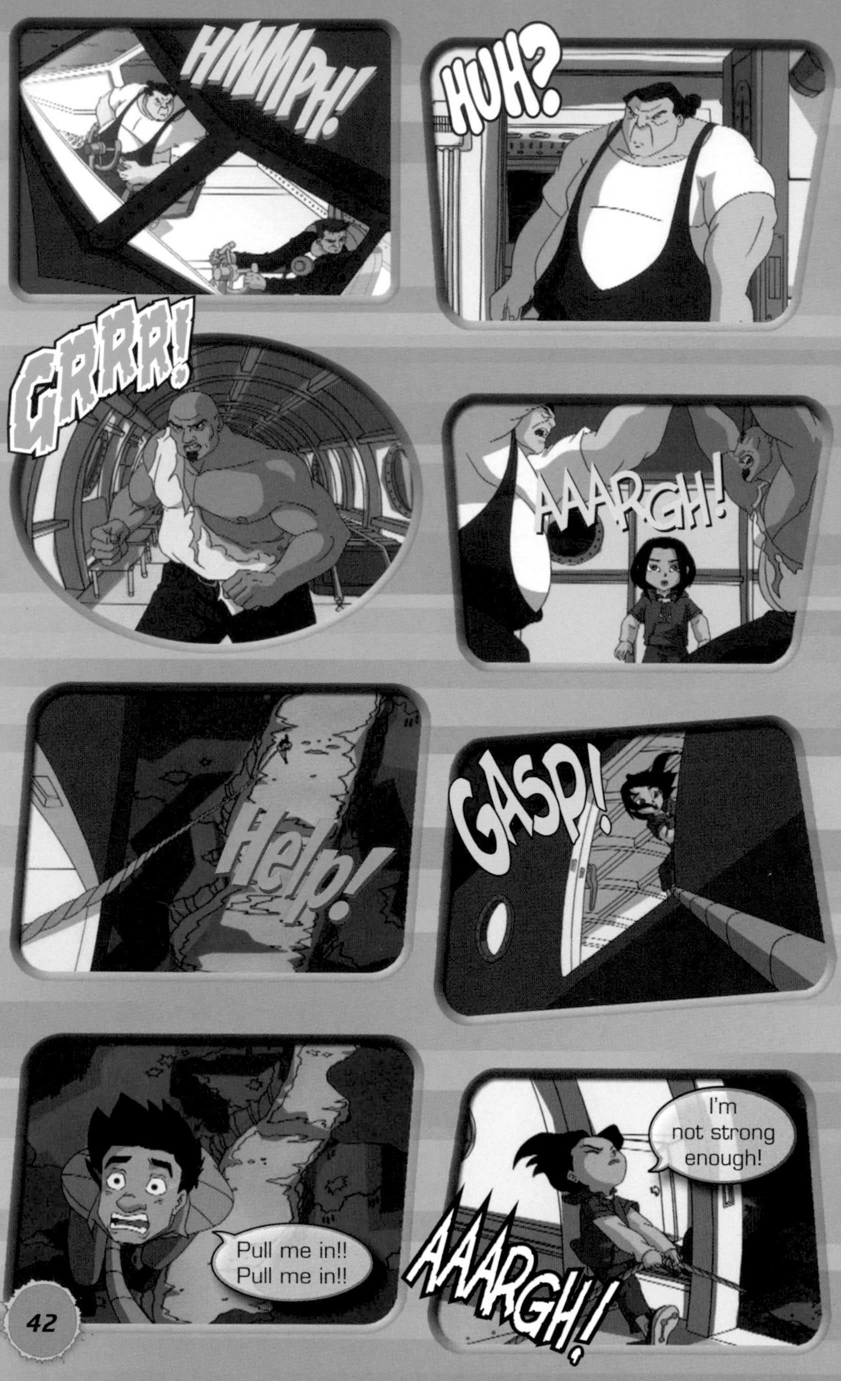
HMMPH!
HUH?
GRRR!
AAARGH!
Help!
GASP!
Pull me in!!
Pull me in!!
I'm not strong enough!
AAARGH!

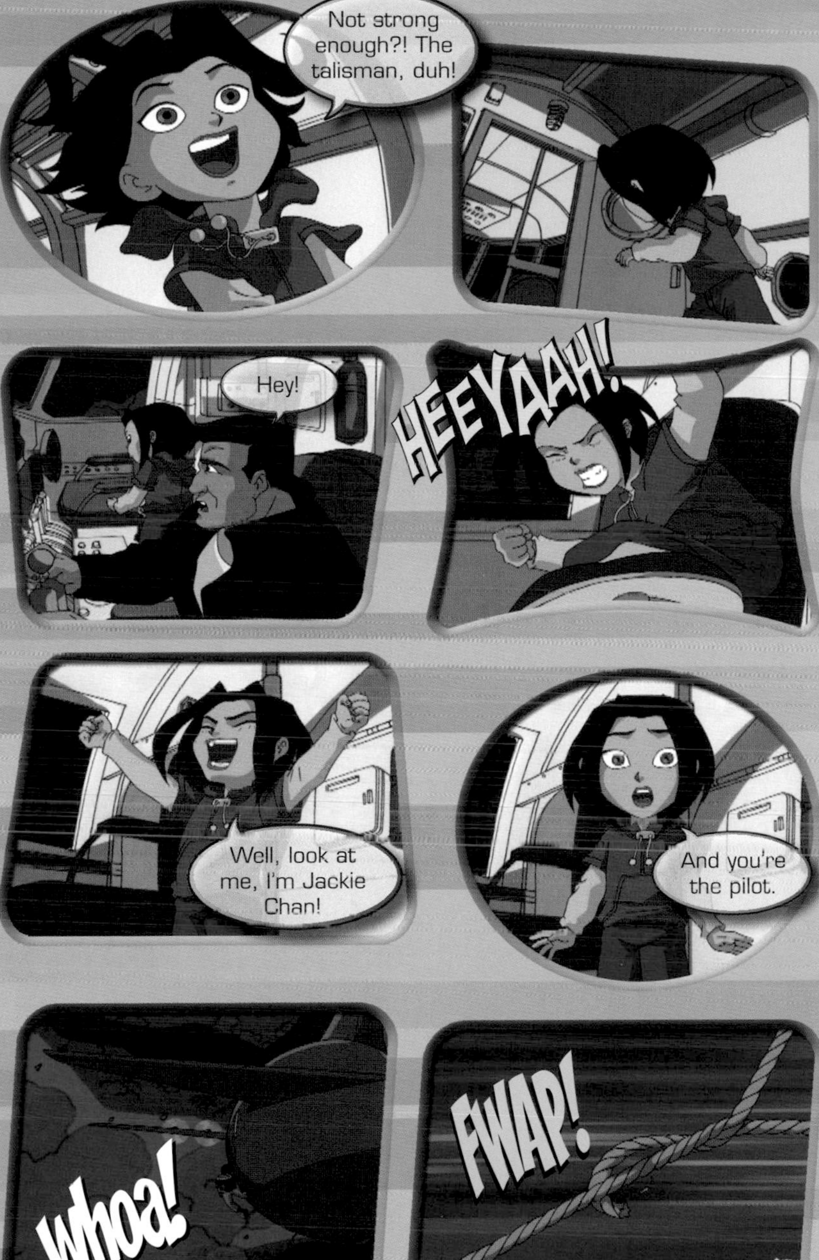
Not strong enough?! The talisman, duh!
Hey!
HEEYAAH!
Well, look at me, I'm Jackie Chan!
And you're the pilot.
Whoa!
FWAP!

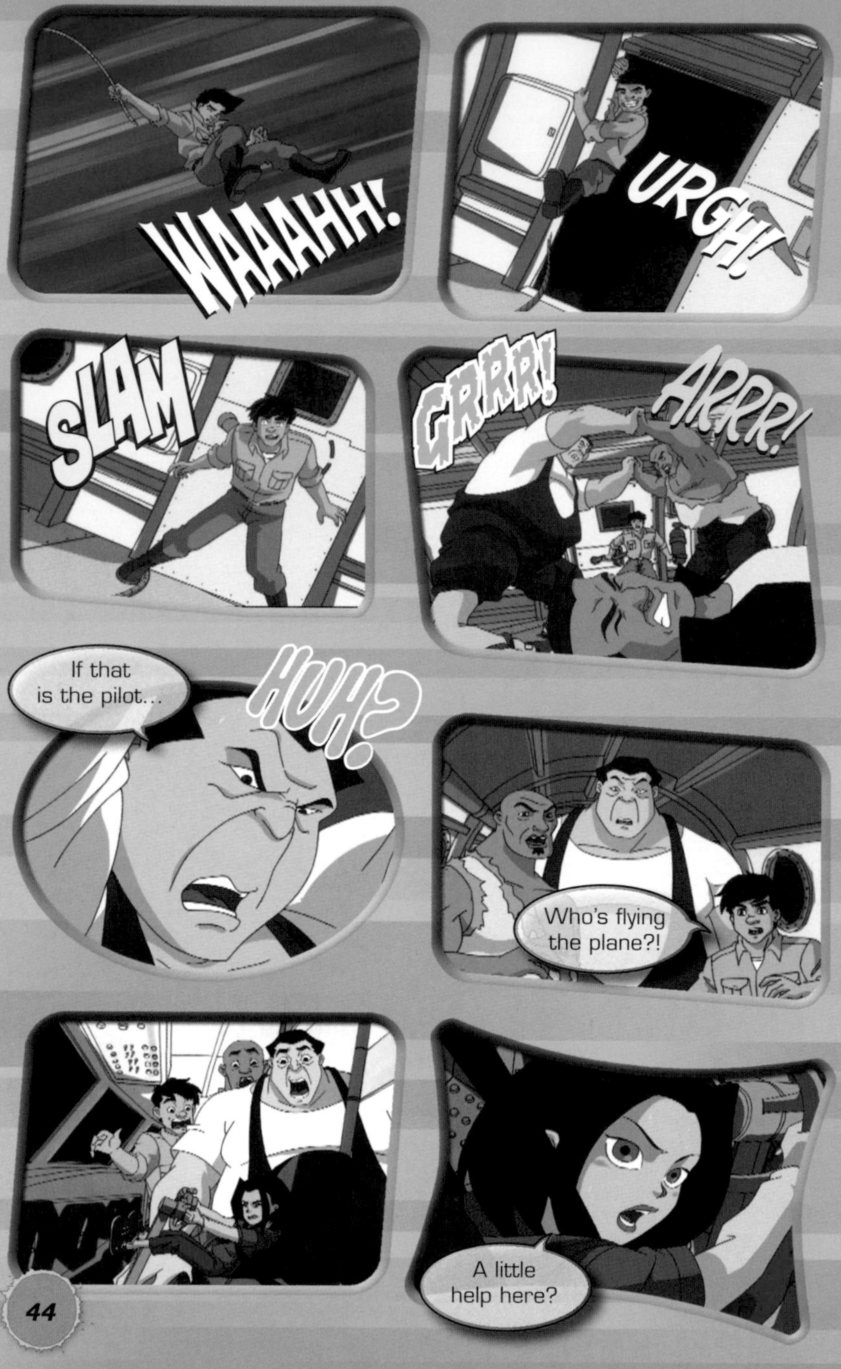
WAAAHH!
URGH!
SLAM
GRRR!
ARRR!
If that is the pilot...
HUH?
Who's flying the plane?!
A little help here?

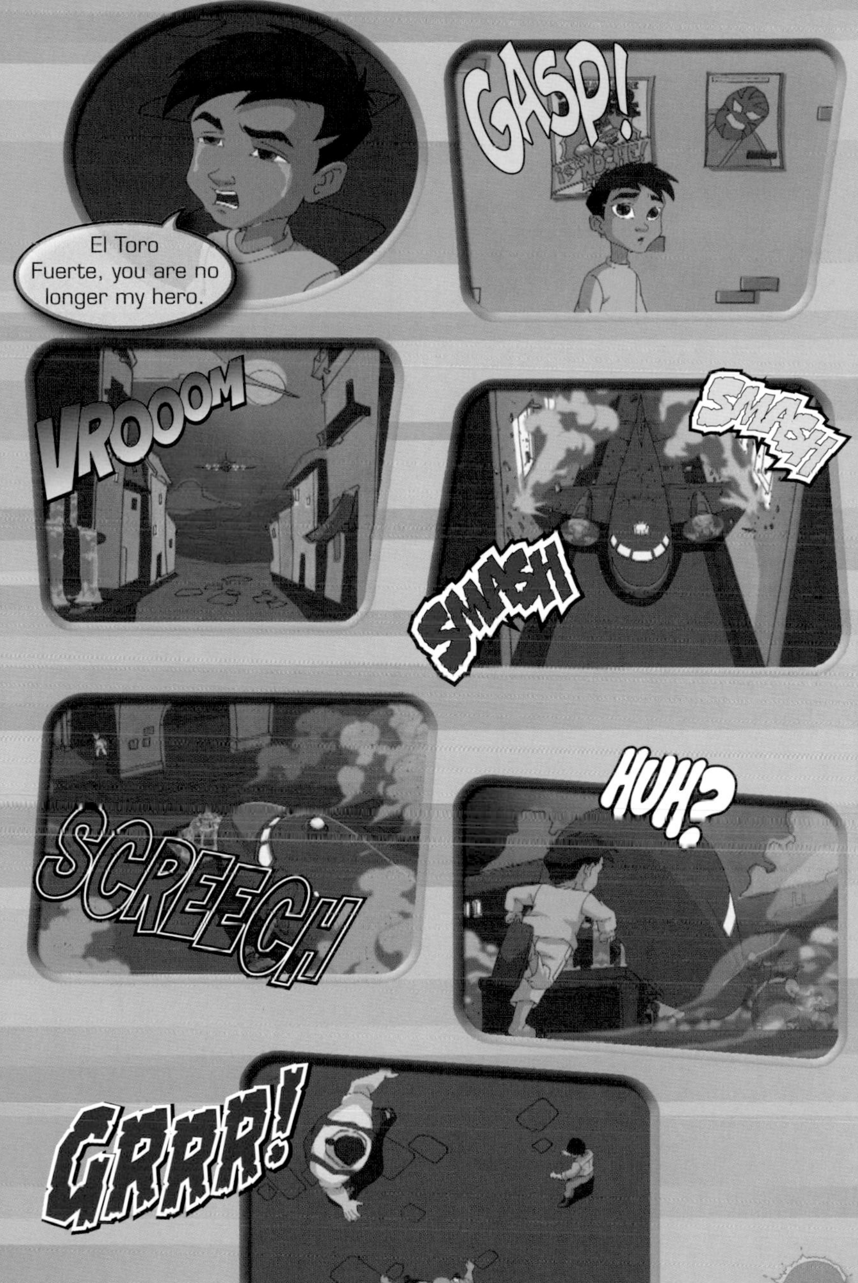
El Toro Fuerte, you are no longer my hero.
GASP!
VROOOM
SMASH
SMASH
SCREECH
HUH?
GRRR!

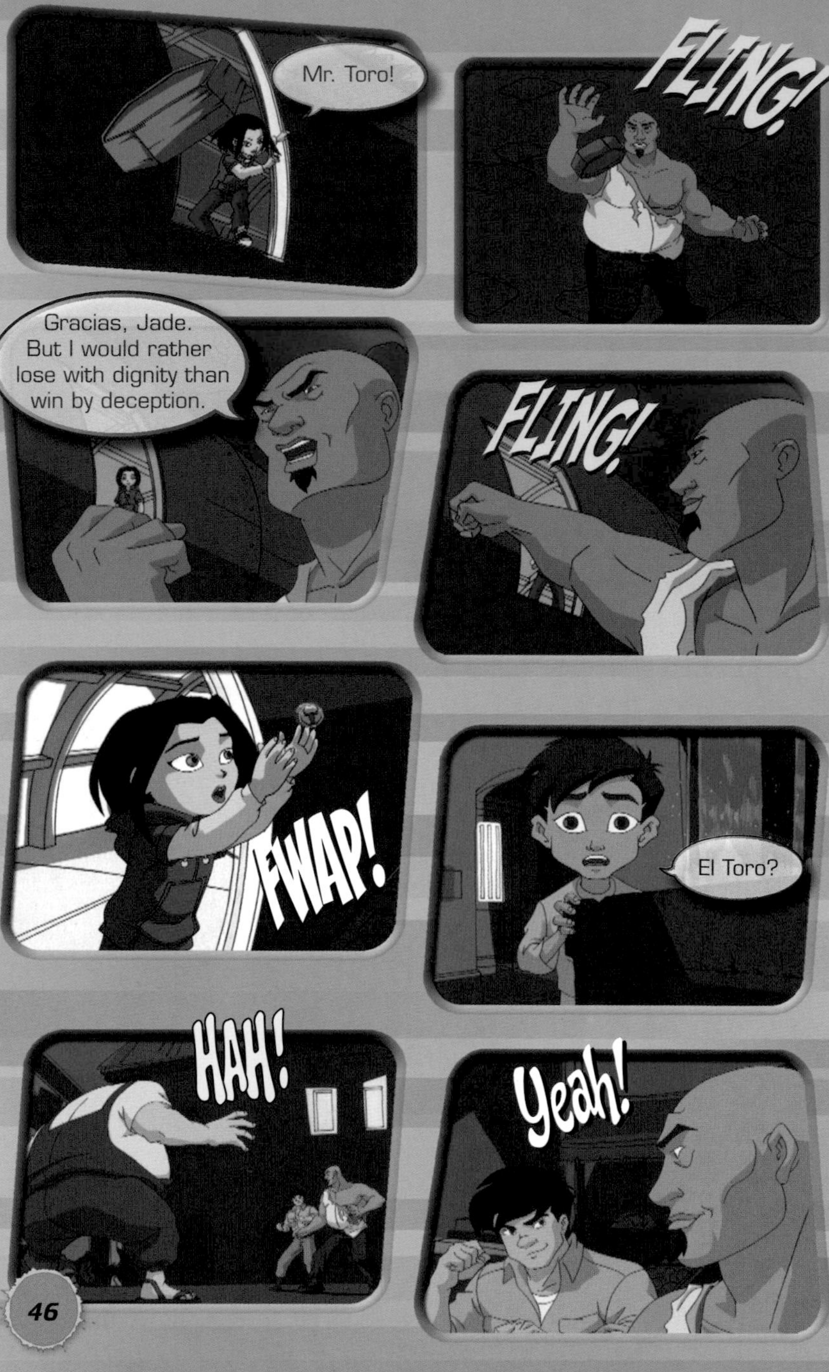
Mr. Toro!
FLING!
Gracias, Jade. But I would rather lose with dignity than win by deception.
FLING!
FWAP!
El Toro?
HAH!
Yeah!

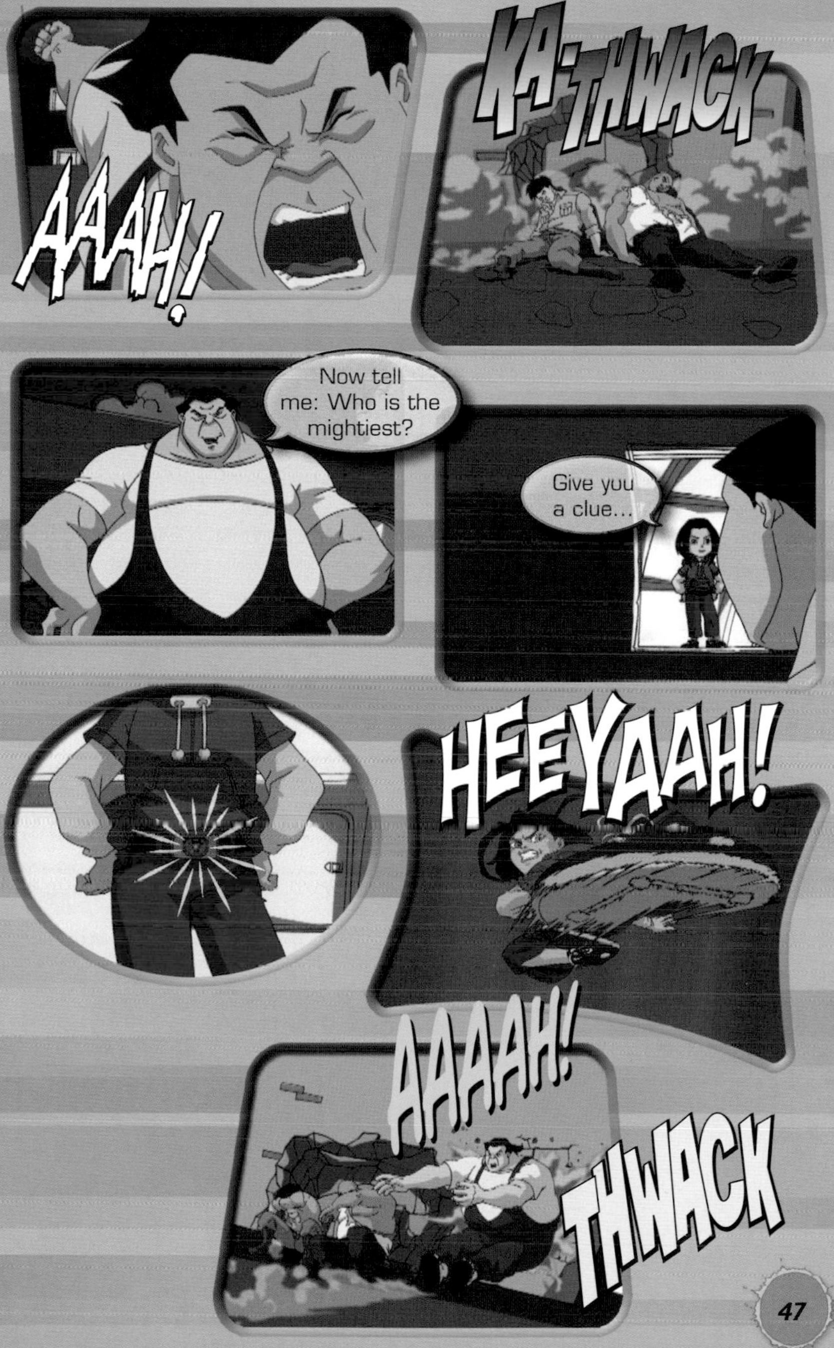
AAAH!
KA-THWACK
Now tell me: Who is the mightiest?
Give you a clue...
HEEYAAH!
AAAAH!
THWACK

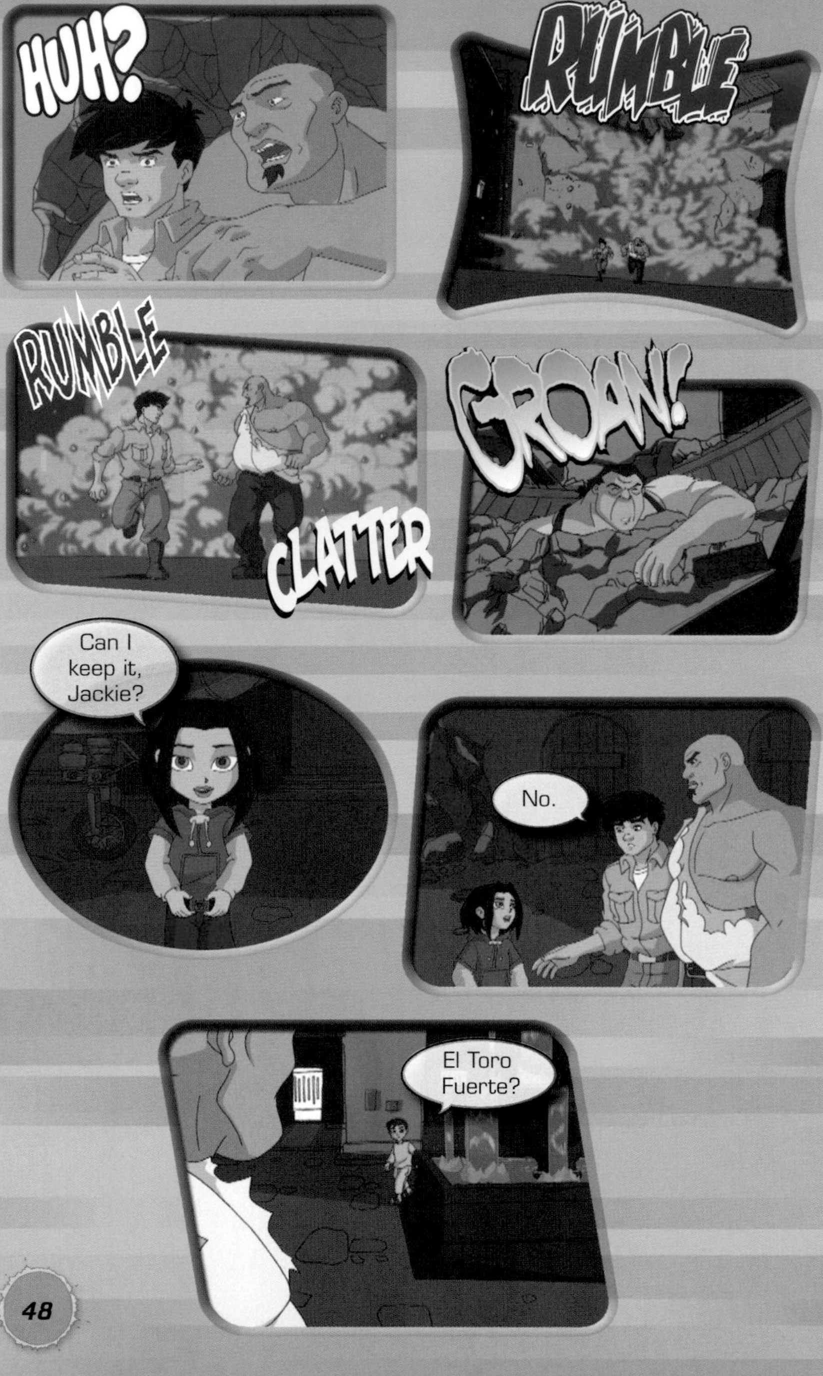
HUH?
RUMBLE
RUMBLE
CLATTER
GROAN!
Can I keep it, Jackie?
No.
El Toro Fuerte?

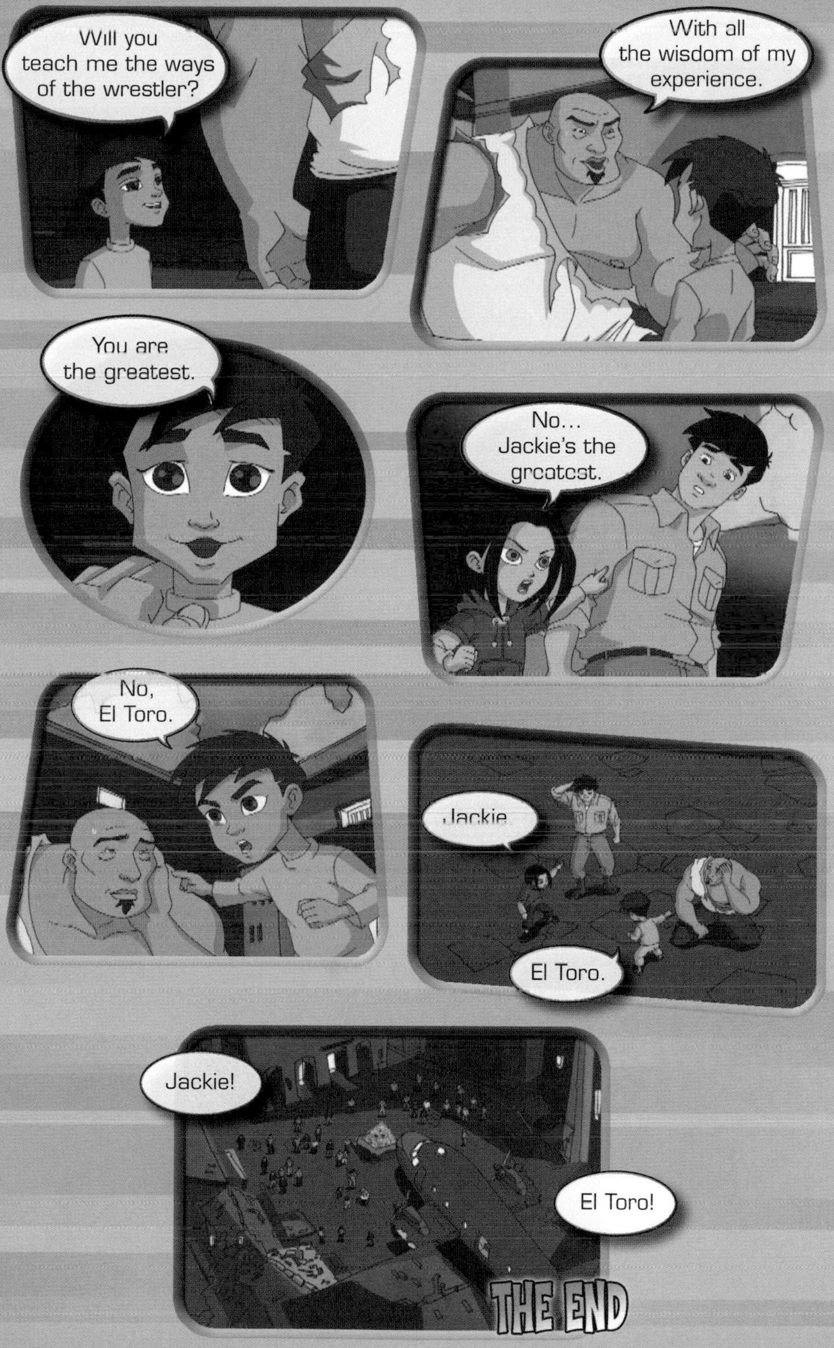
Will you teach me the ways of the wrestler?
With all the wisdom of my experience.
You are the greatest.
No... Jackie's the greatest.
No, El Toro.
Jackie.
El Toro.
Jackie!
El Toro!
THE END

JACKIE CHAN ADVENTURES.

ENTER...THE VIPER

WRITTEN BY
DAVID SLACK

Please, you must let me have the talisman...

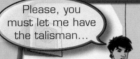

It is only a matter of time before The Dark Hand tries to steal it!

We do so appreciate the warning, Mister...Chan, was it?

However, we protect the world-famous Pink Puma diamond. If we can guard a gem like that, I am sure that your "Dark Hand" will present no serious threat.

WHIR

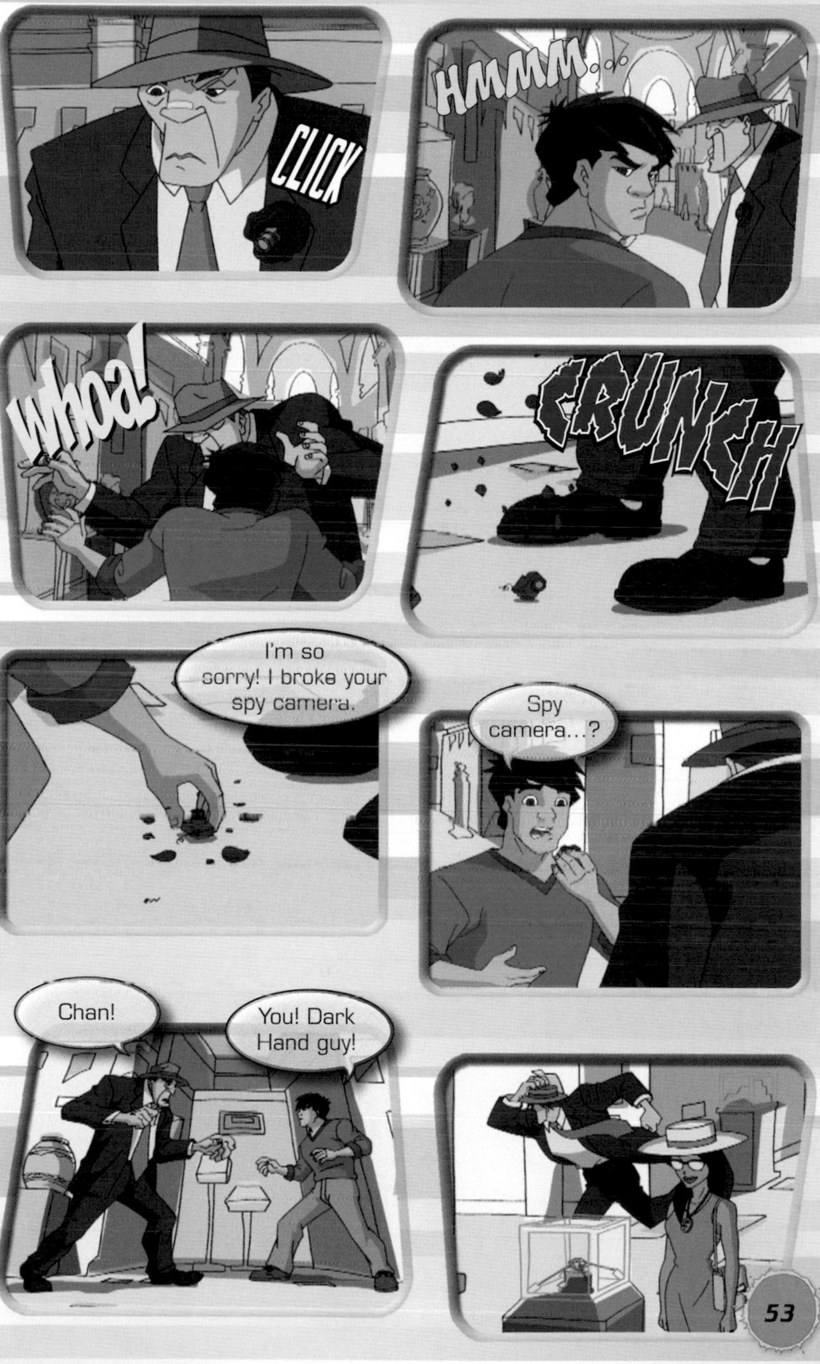
CLICK
HMMM...
whoa!
CRUNCH
I'm so sorry! I broke your spy camera.
Spy camera...?
Chan!
You! Dark Hand guy!

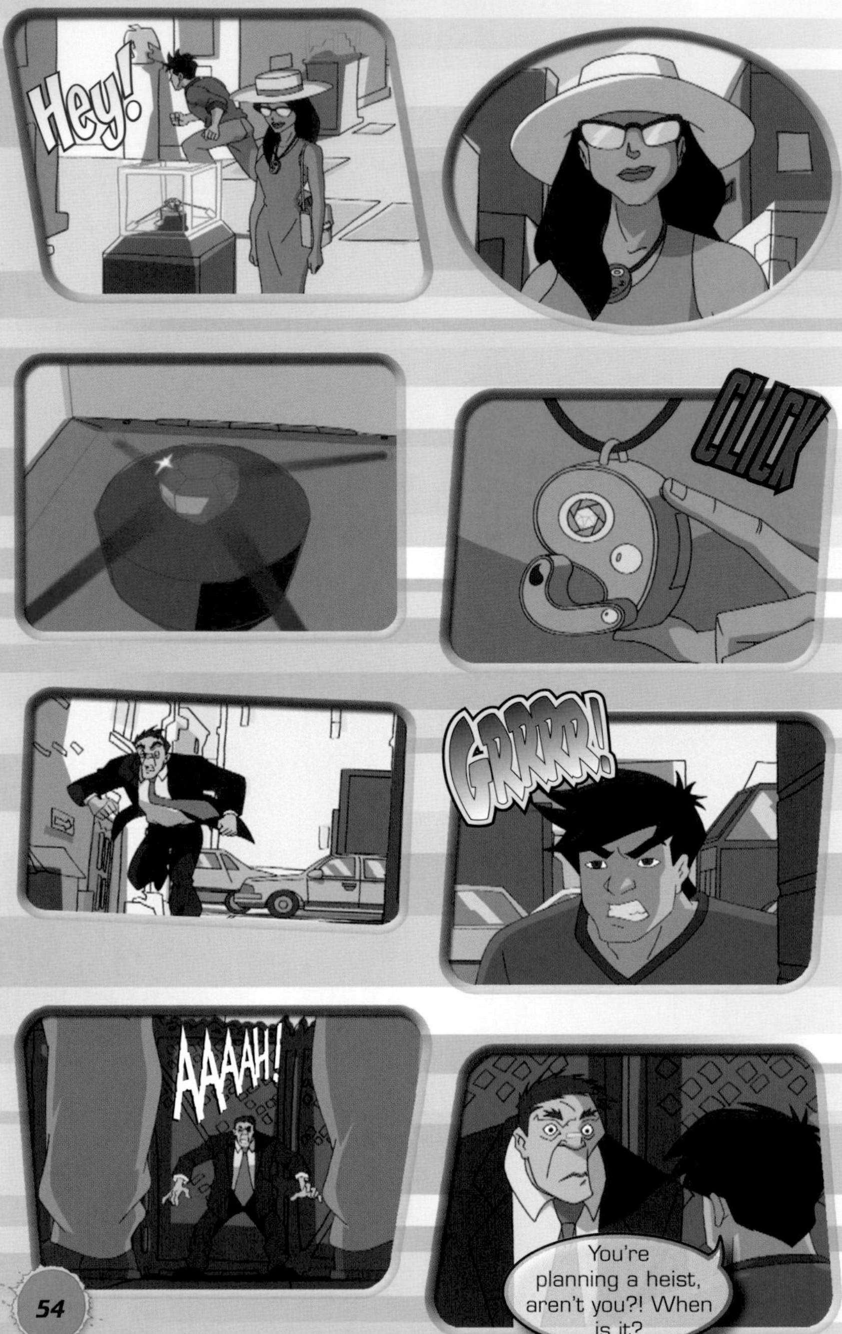
Hey!
CLICK
GRRRR!
AAAAH!
You're planning a heist, aren't you?! When is it?

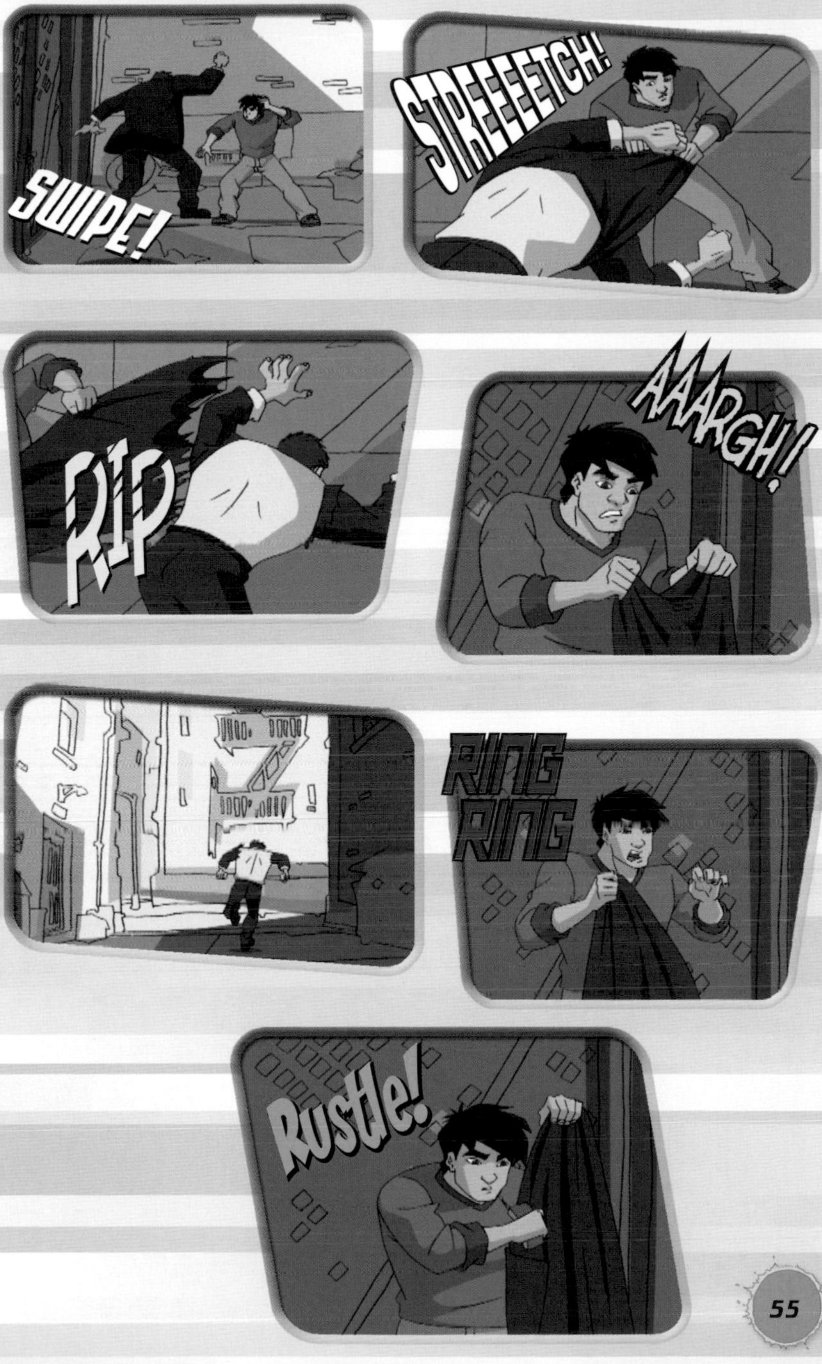
SWIPE!
STREEEEETCH!
RIP
AAARGH!
RING
RING
Rustle!

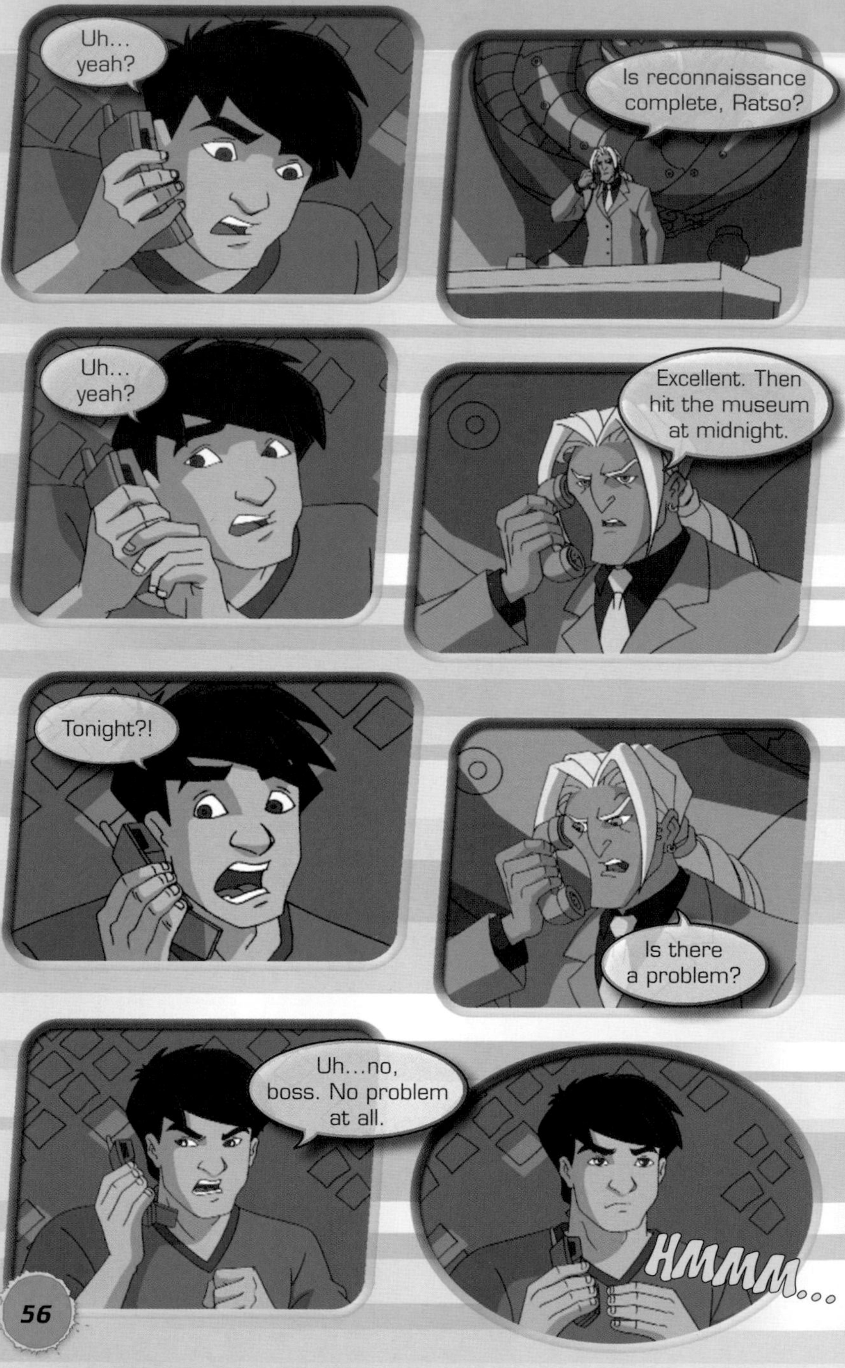

Uh... yeah?
Is reconnaissance complete, Ratso?
Uh... yeah?
Excellent. Then hit the museum at midnight.
Tonight?!
Is there a problem?
Uh...no, boss. No problem at all.
HMMM...

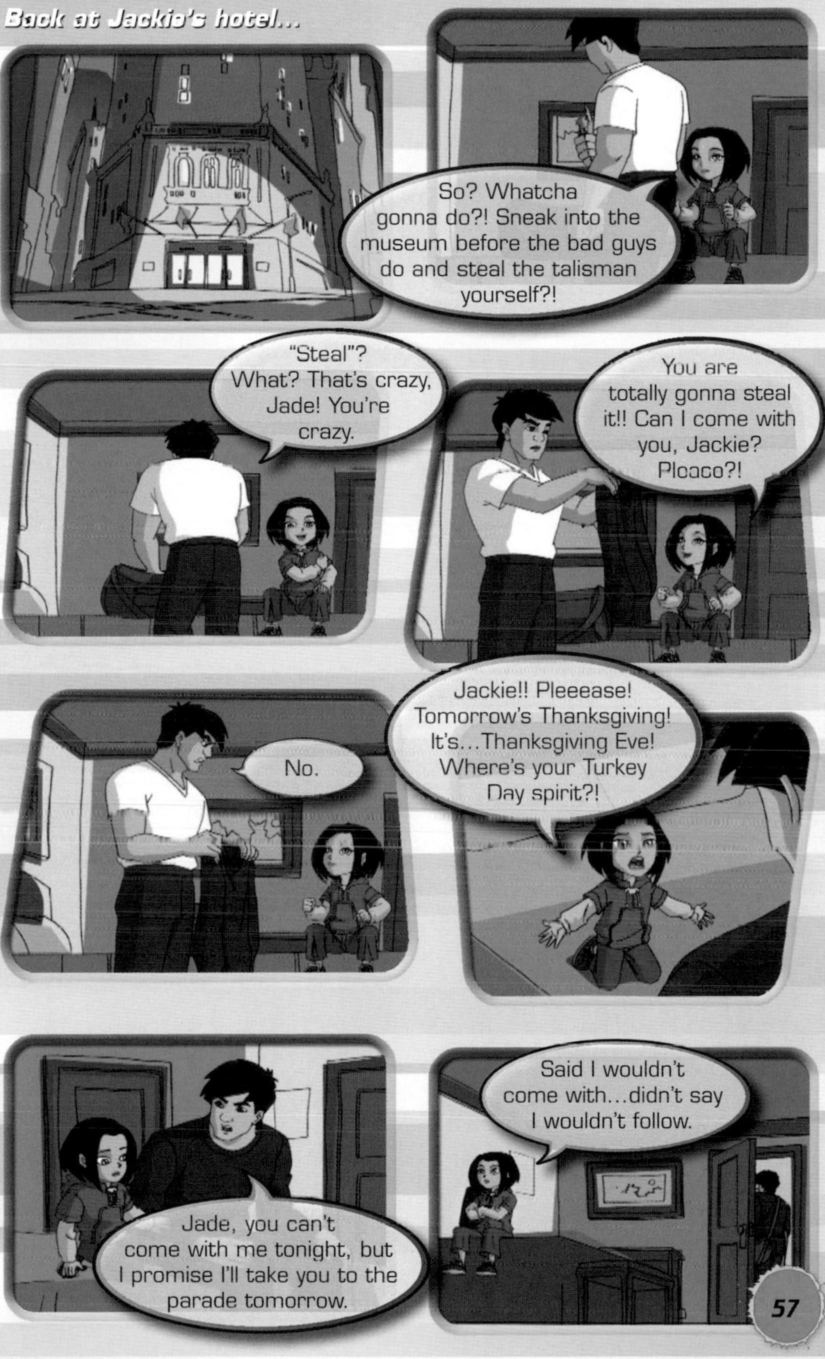
Back at Jackie's hotel...
So? Whatcha gonna do?! Sneak into the museum before the bad guys do and steal the talisman yourself?!
"Steal"? What? That's crazy, Jade! You're crazy.
You are totally gonna steal it!! Can I come with you, Jackie? Please?!
No.
Jackie!! Pleeease! Tomorrow's Thanksgiving! It's...Thanksgiving Eve! Where's your Turkey Day spirit?!
Jade, you can't come with me tonight, but I promise I'll take you to the parade tomorrow.
Said I wouldn't come with...didn't say I wouldn't follow.

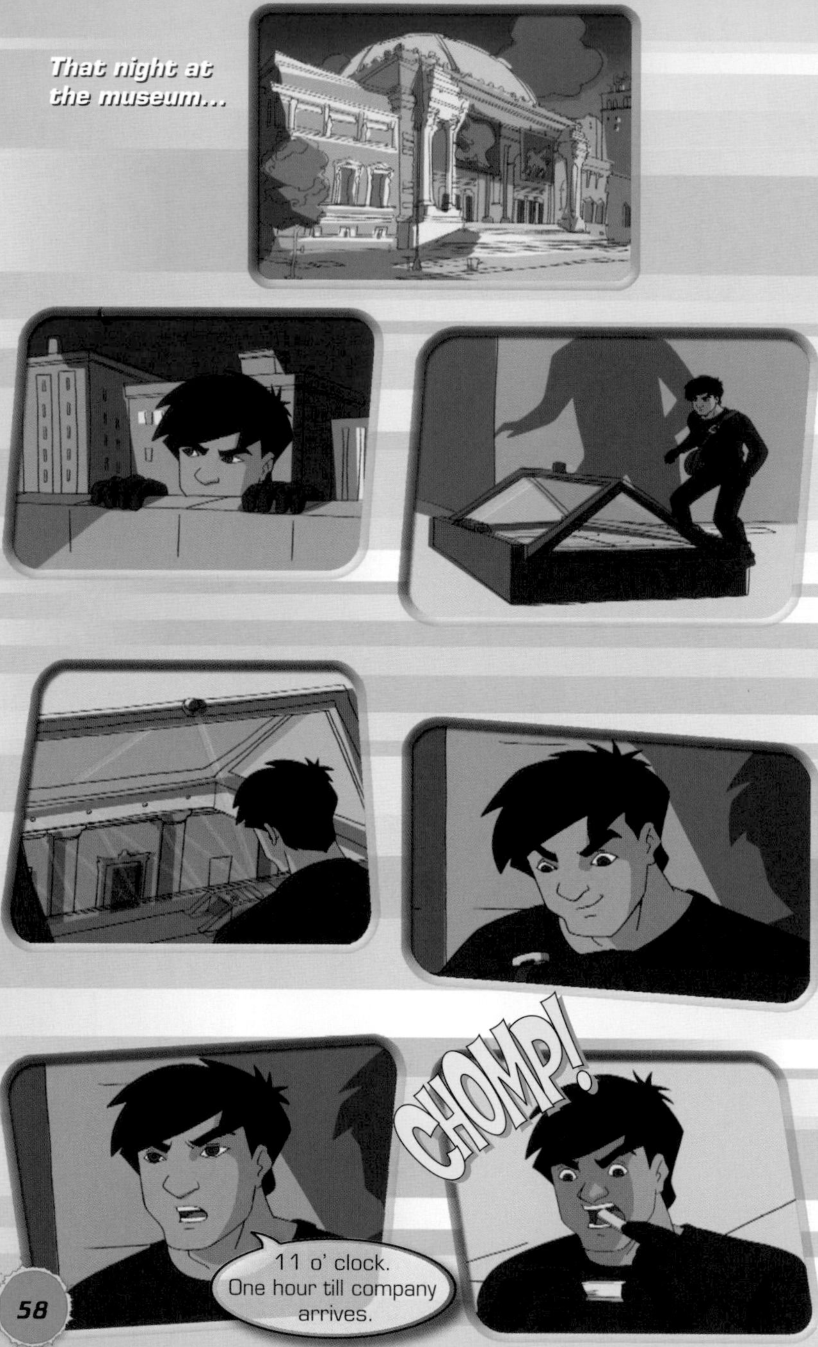
That night at the museum...
CHOMP!
11 o' clock.
One hour till company arrives.

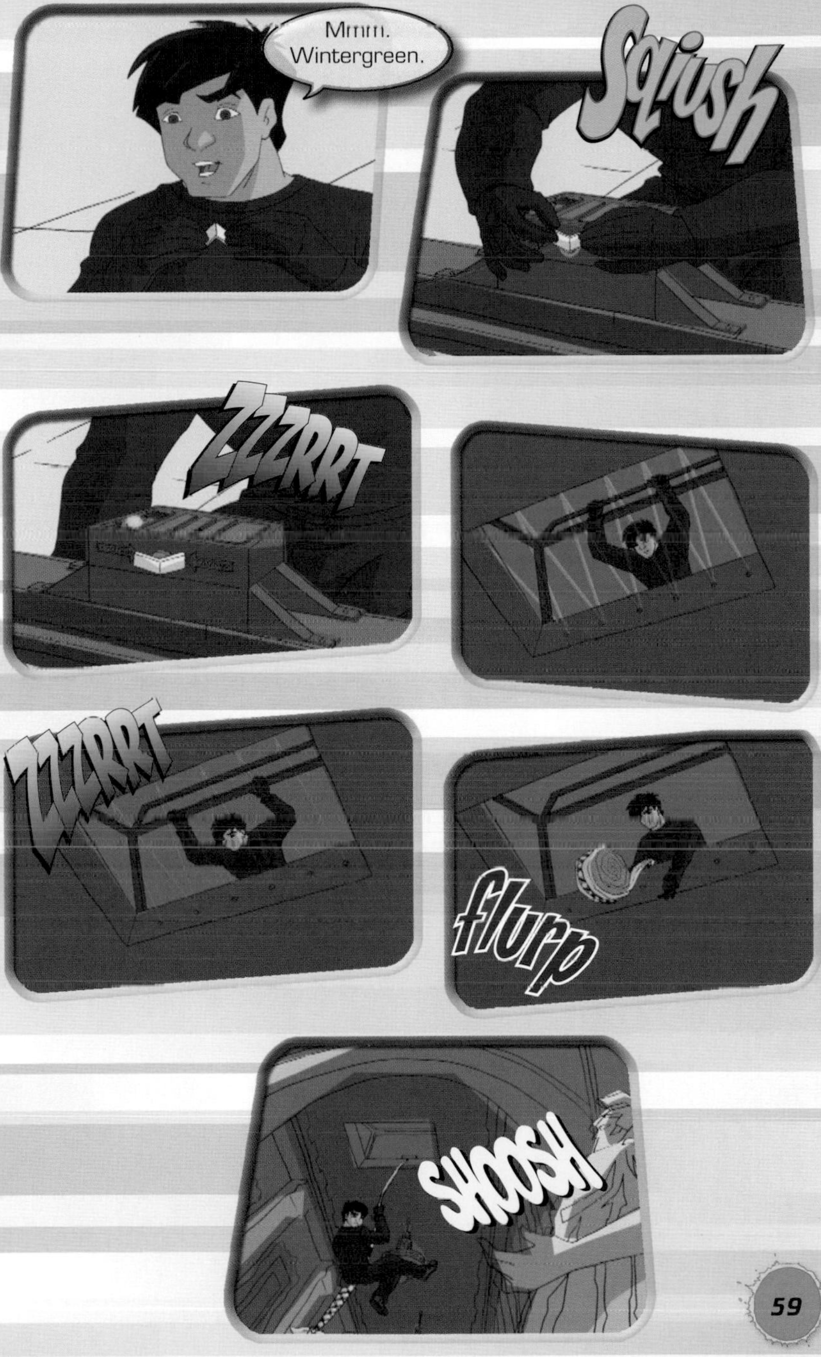
Mmm.
Wintergreen.
Sqiush
ZZZRRT
ZZZRRT
flurp
SHOOSH

Meanwhile...

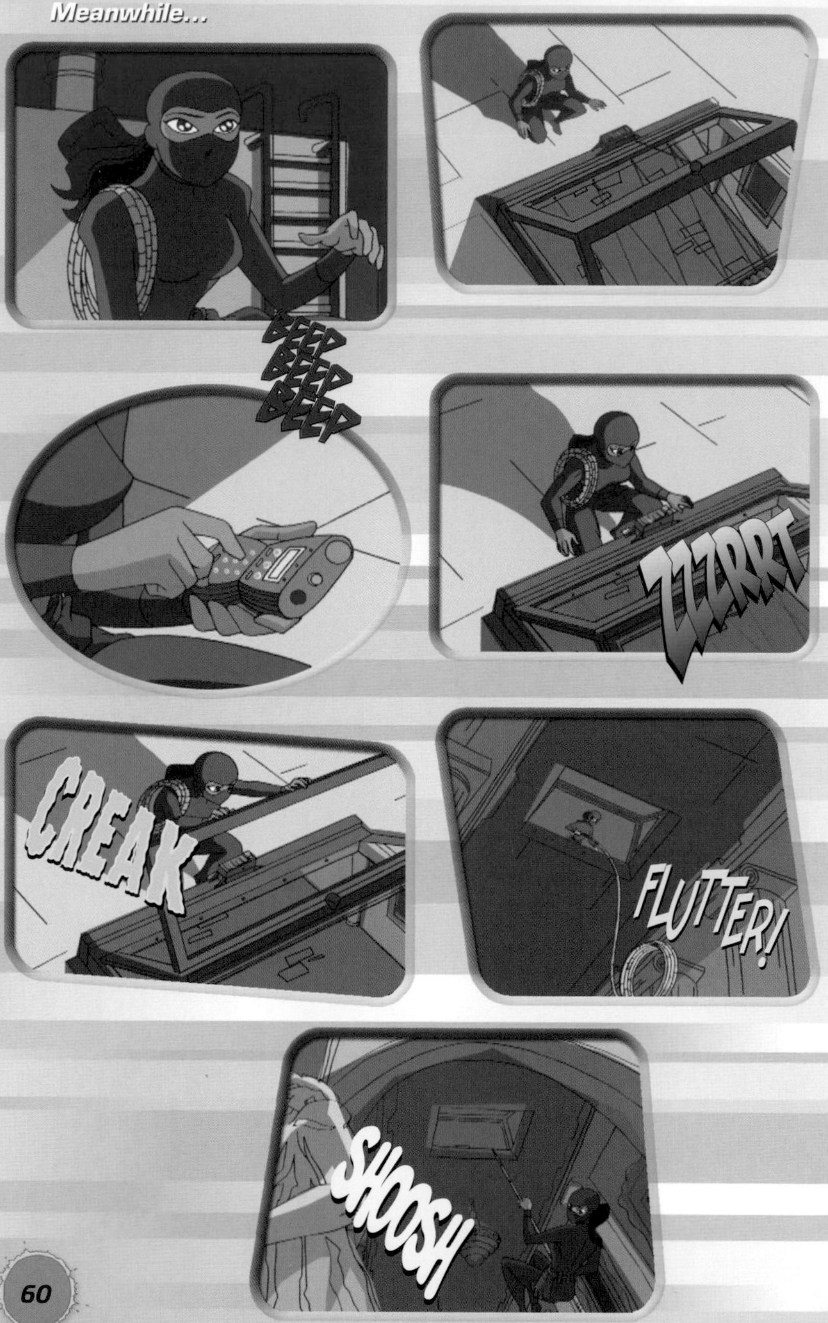
BEEP
BEEP
BEEP
ZZZRRT
CREAK
FLUTTER!
SHOOSH

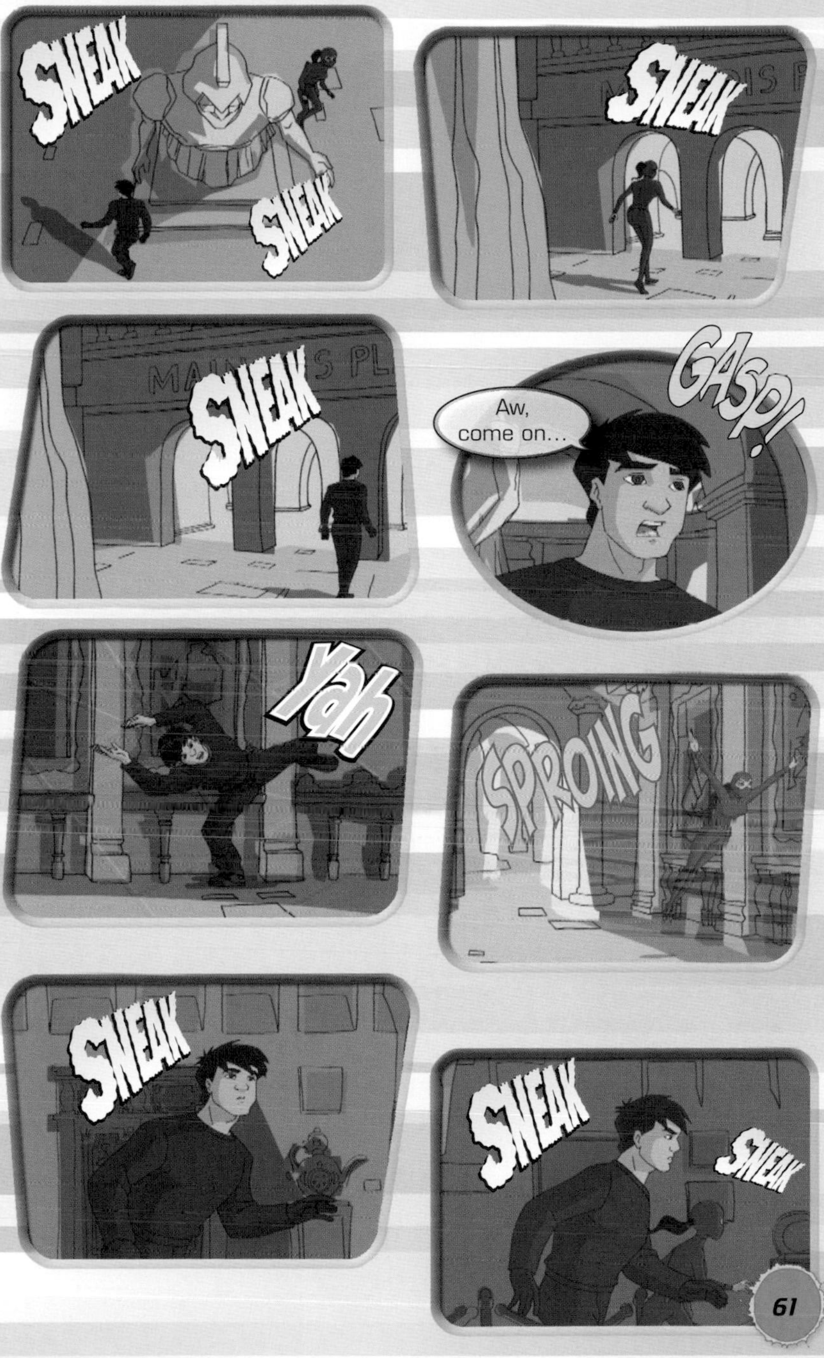

SNEAK
SNEAK
SNEAK
SNEAK
Aw, come on...
GASP!
Yah
SPROING
SNEAK
SNEAK
SNEAK

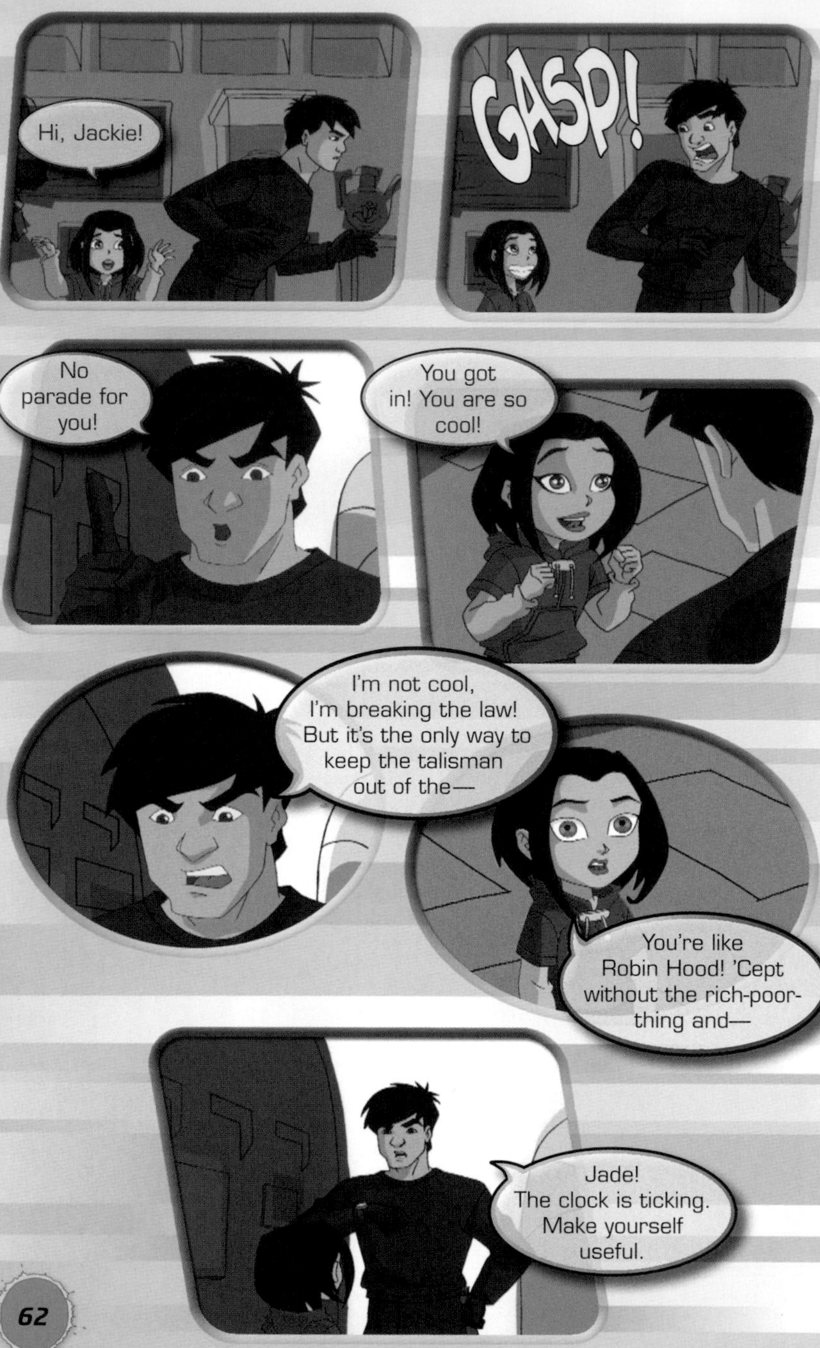
Hi, Jackie!
GASP!
No parade for you!
You got in! You are so cool!
I'm not cool, I'm breaking the law! But it's the only way to keep the talisman out of the—
You're like Robin Hood! 'Cept without the rich-poor-thing and—
Jade! The clock is ticking. Make yourself useful.

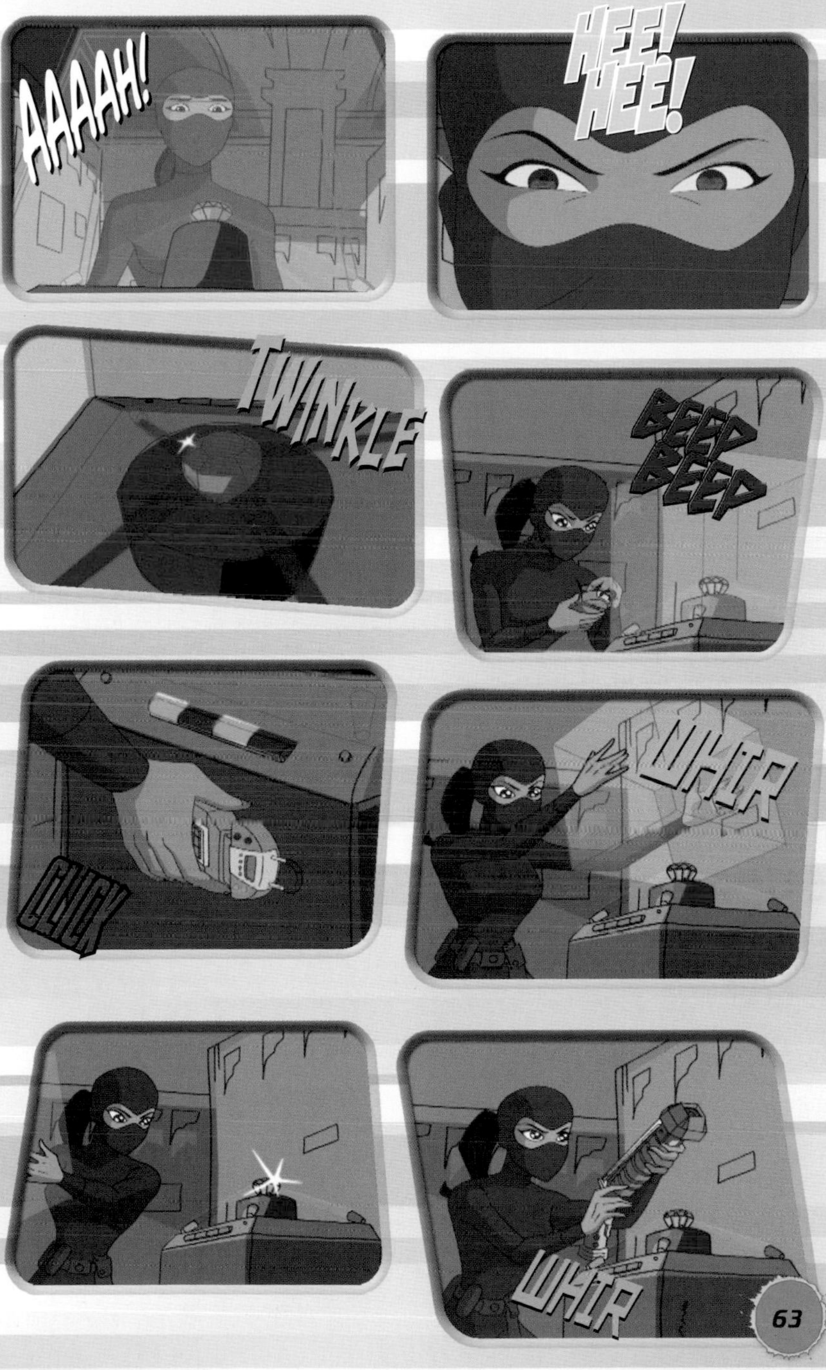
AAAAH!
HEE! HEE!
TWINKLE
BEEP BEEP
CLICK
WHIR
WHIR

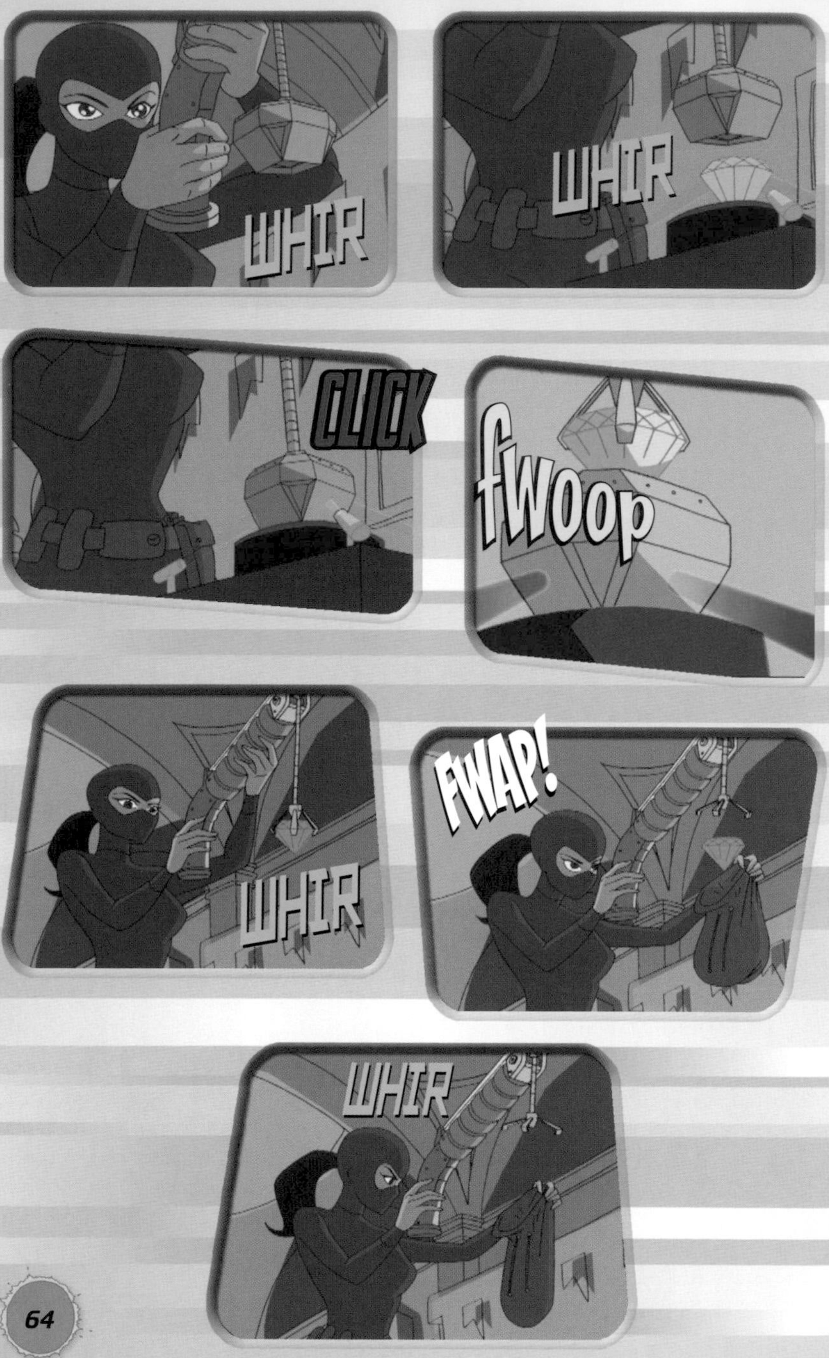
WHIR
WHIR
CLICK
fWOOp
WHIR
FWAP!
WHIR

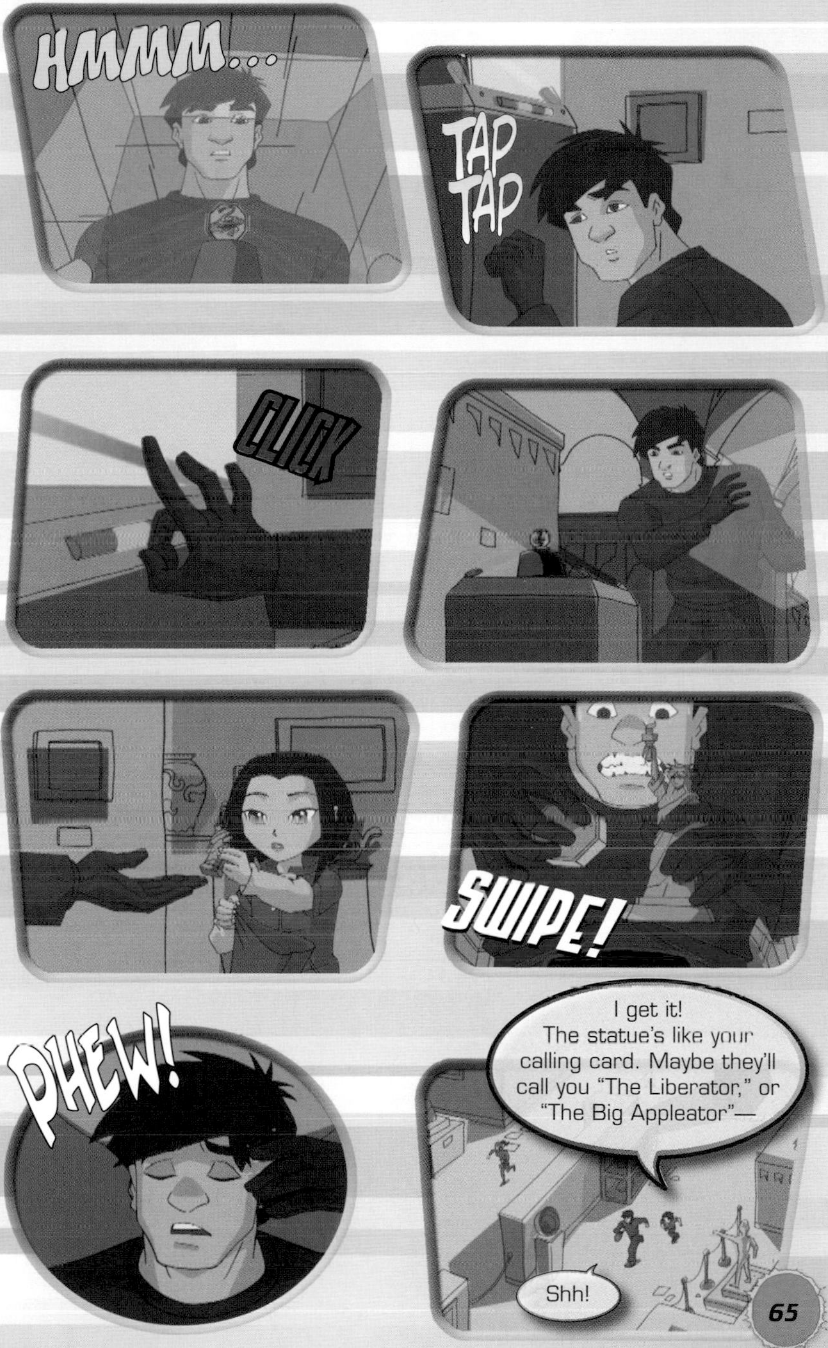
HMMM...
TAP TAP
CLICK
SWIPE!
PHEW!
I get it! The statue's like your calling card. Maybe they'll call you "The Liberator," or "The Big Appleator"—
Shh!

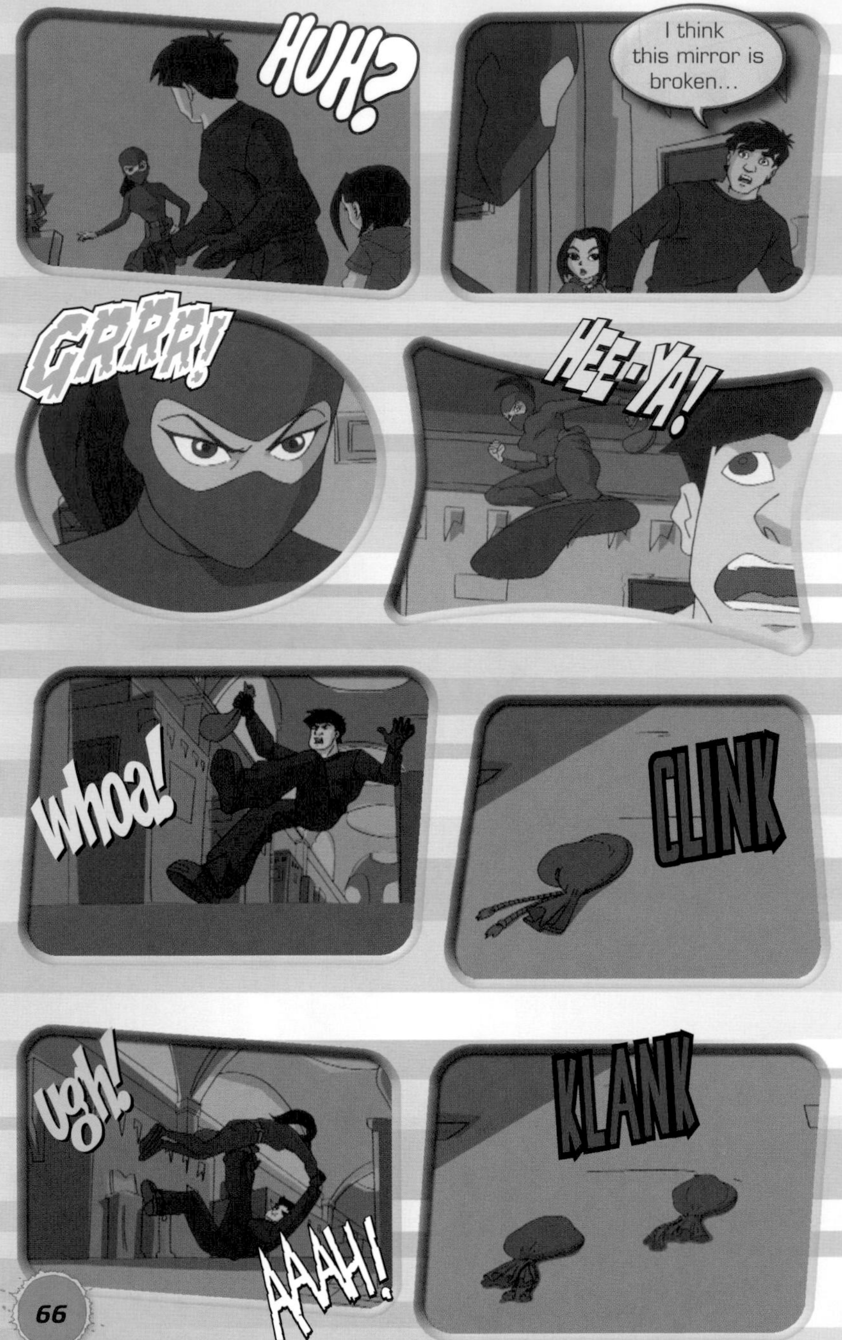
HUH?
I think this mirror is broken...
GRRR!
HEE-YA!
whoa!
CLINK
ugh!
AAAH!
KLANK

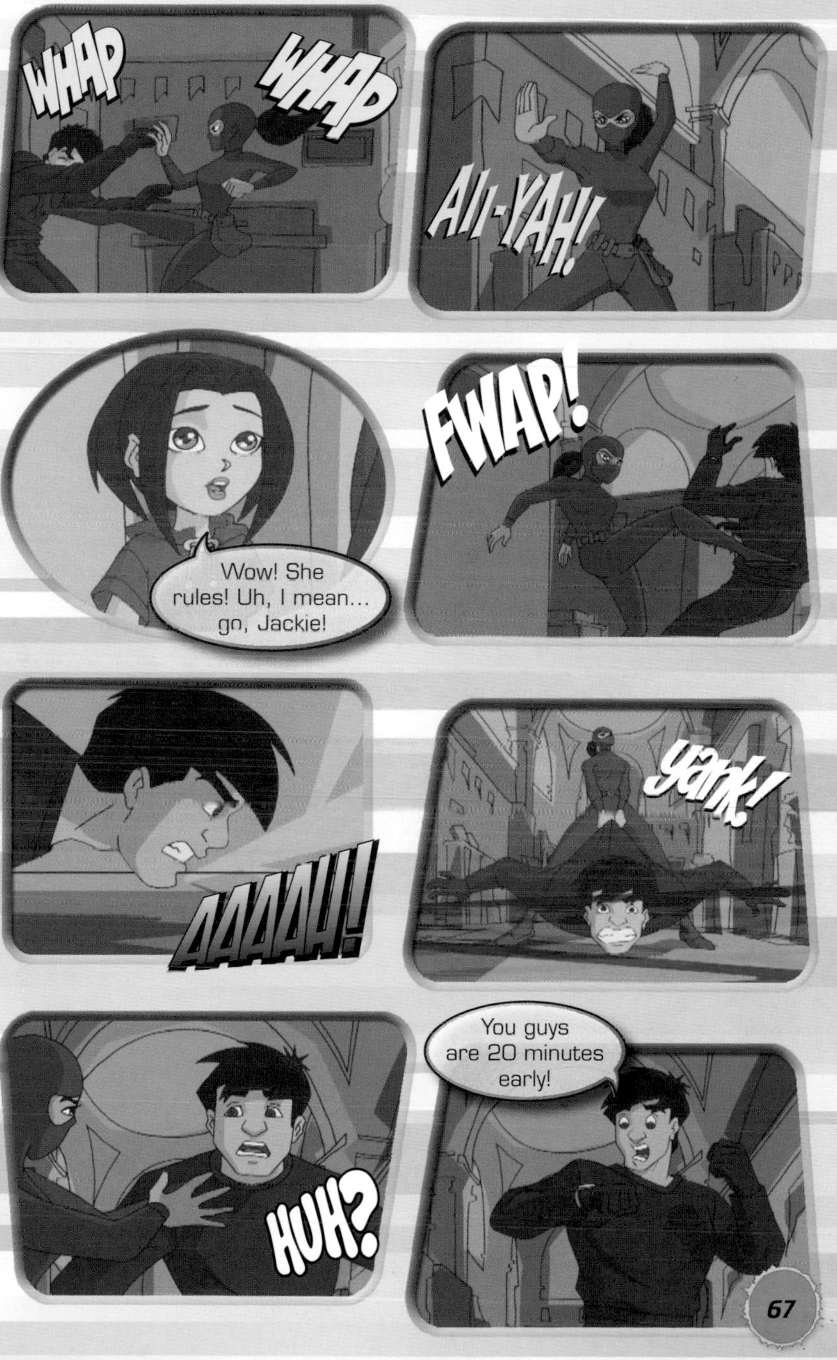
WHAP
WHAP
AII-YAH!
Wow! She rules! Uh, I mean... go, Jackie!
FWAP!
AAAAH!
yank!
HUH?
You guys are 20 minutes early!

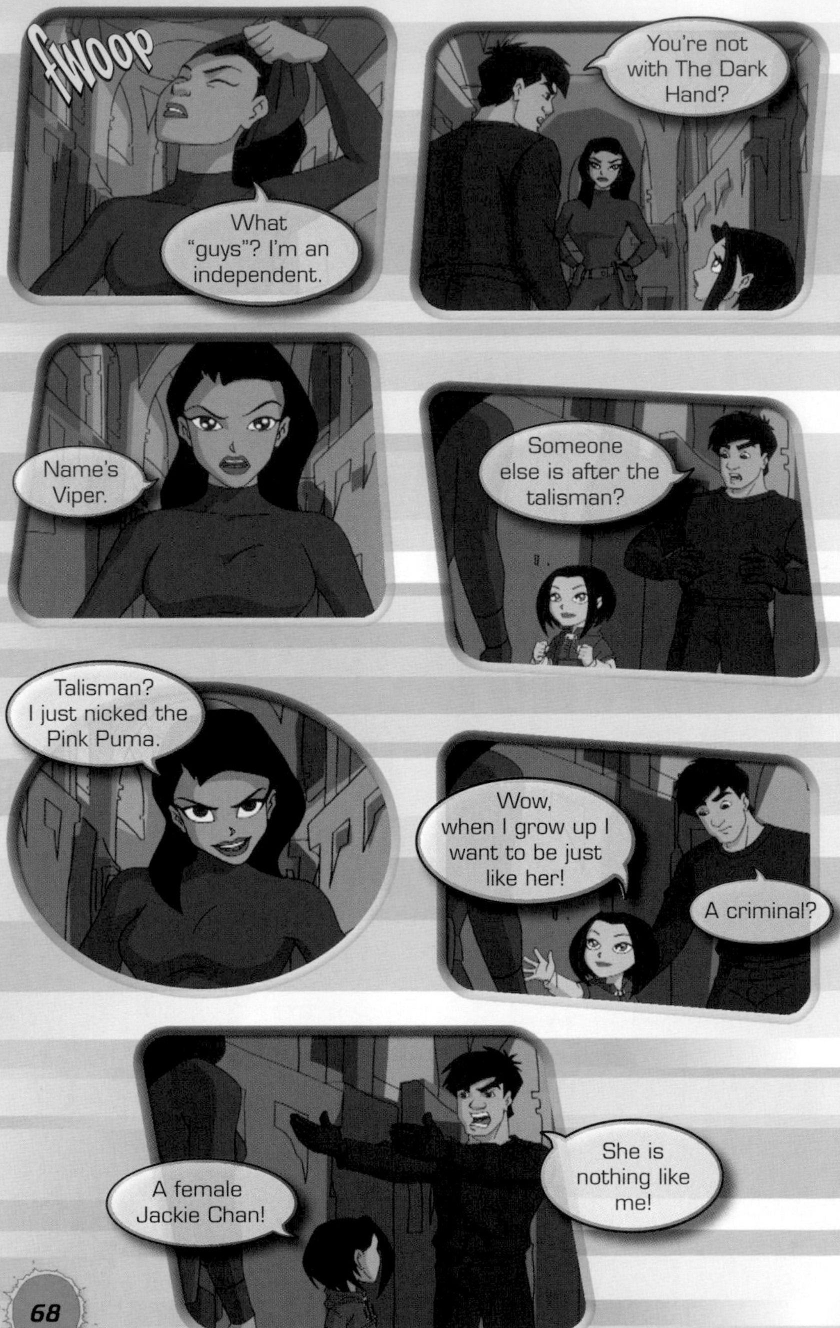
fwoop
What "guys"? I'm an independent.
You're not with The Dark Hand?
Name's Viper.
Someone else is after the talisman?
Talisman? I just nicked the Pink Puma.
Wow, when I grow up I want to be just like her!
A criminal?
A female Jackie Chan!
She is nothing like me!

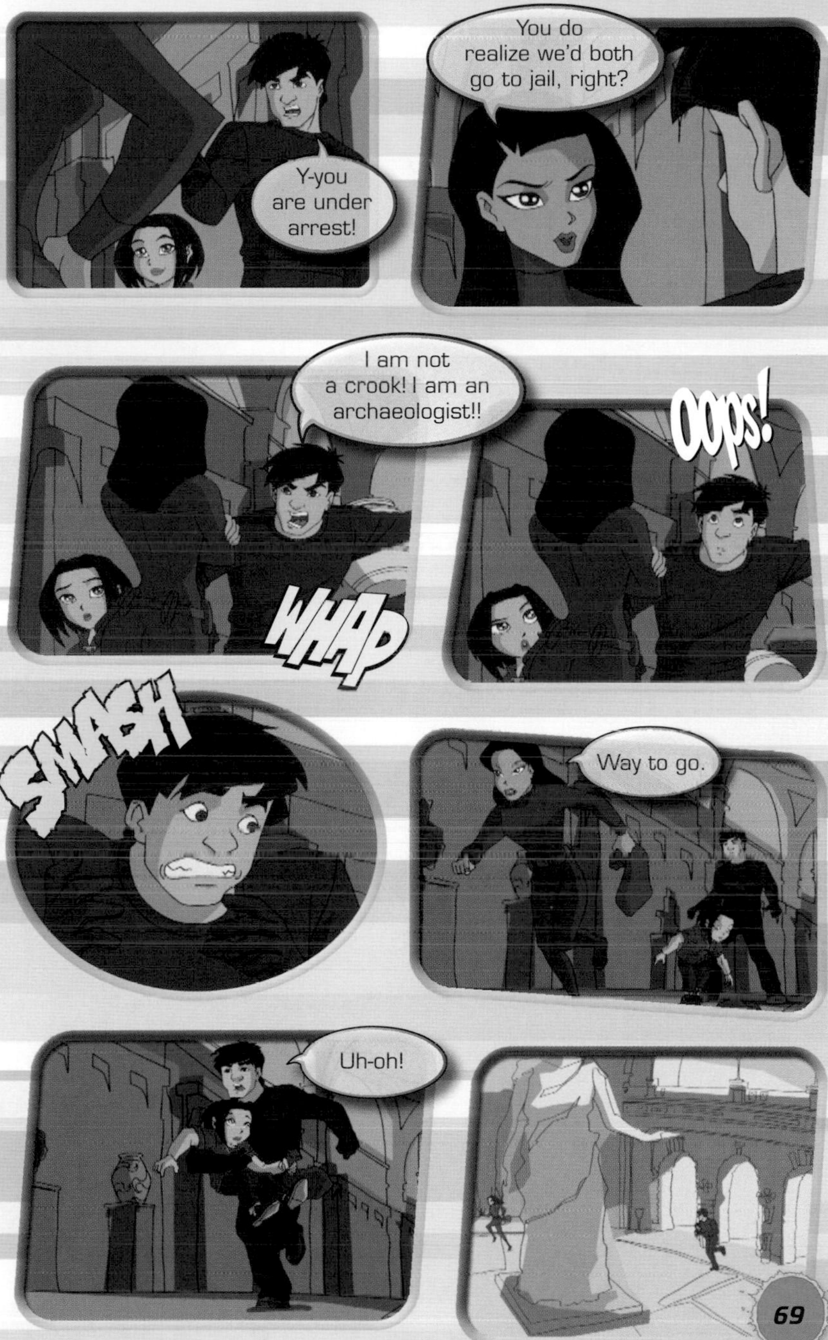

Y-you are under arrest!
You do realize we'd both go to jail, right?
I am not a crook! I am an archaeologist!!
WHAP
OOPS!
SMASH
Way to go.
Uh-oh!

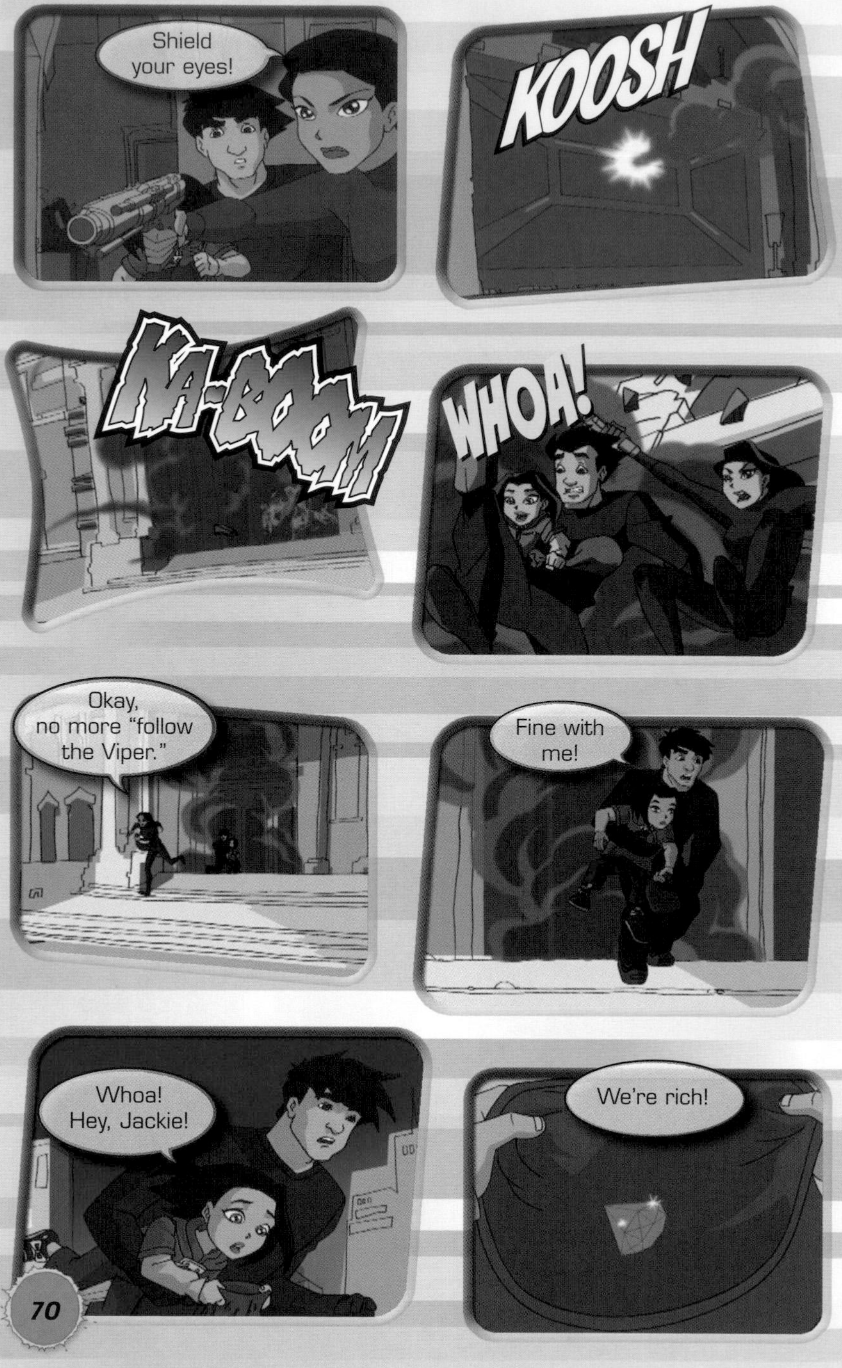
Shield your eyes!
KOOSH
KA-BOOM
WHOA!
Okay, no more "follow the Viper."
Fine with me!
Whoa! Hey, Jackie!
We're rich!

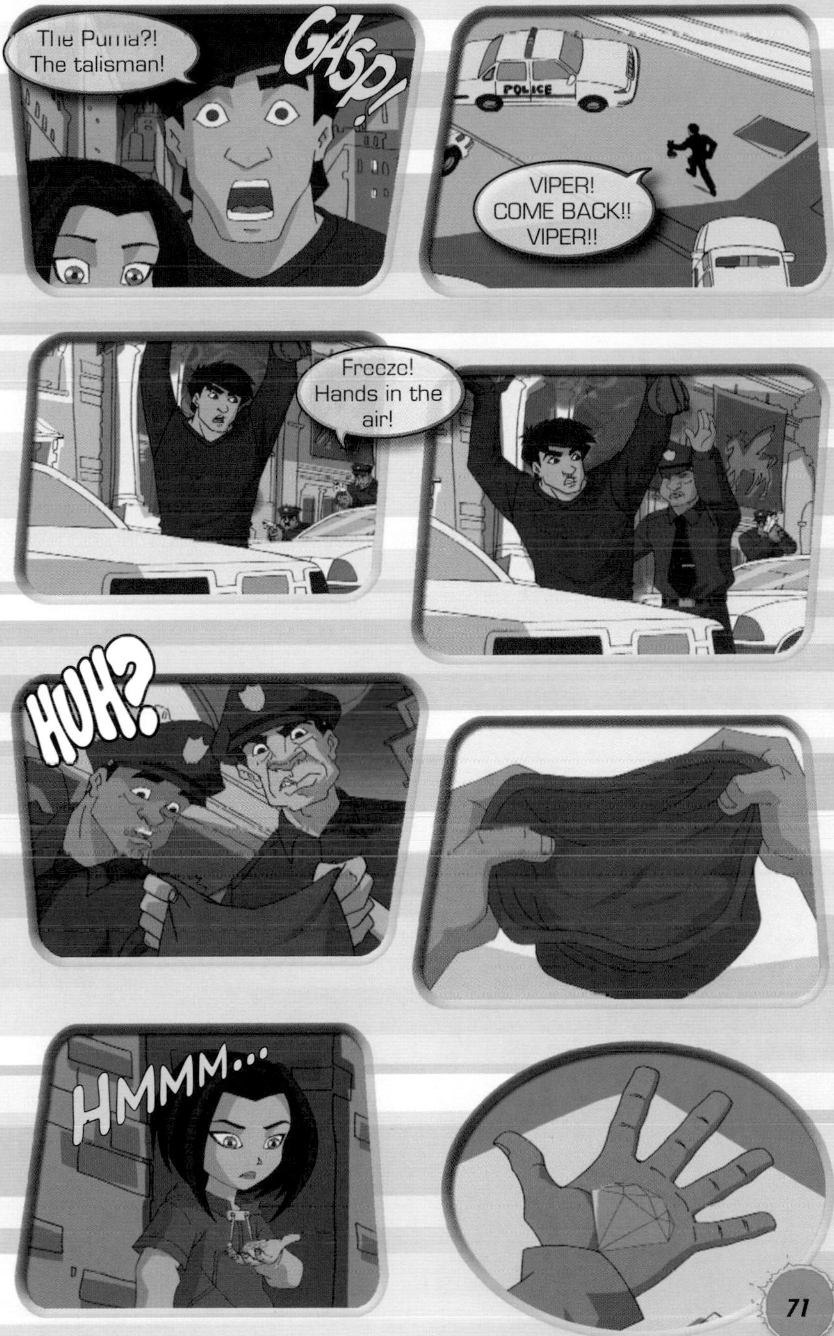
The Puma?!
The talisman!
GASP!
VIPER!
COME BACK!!
VIPER!!
POLICE
Freeze!
Hands in the
air!
HUH?
HMMM...

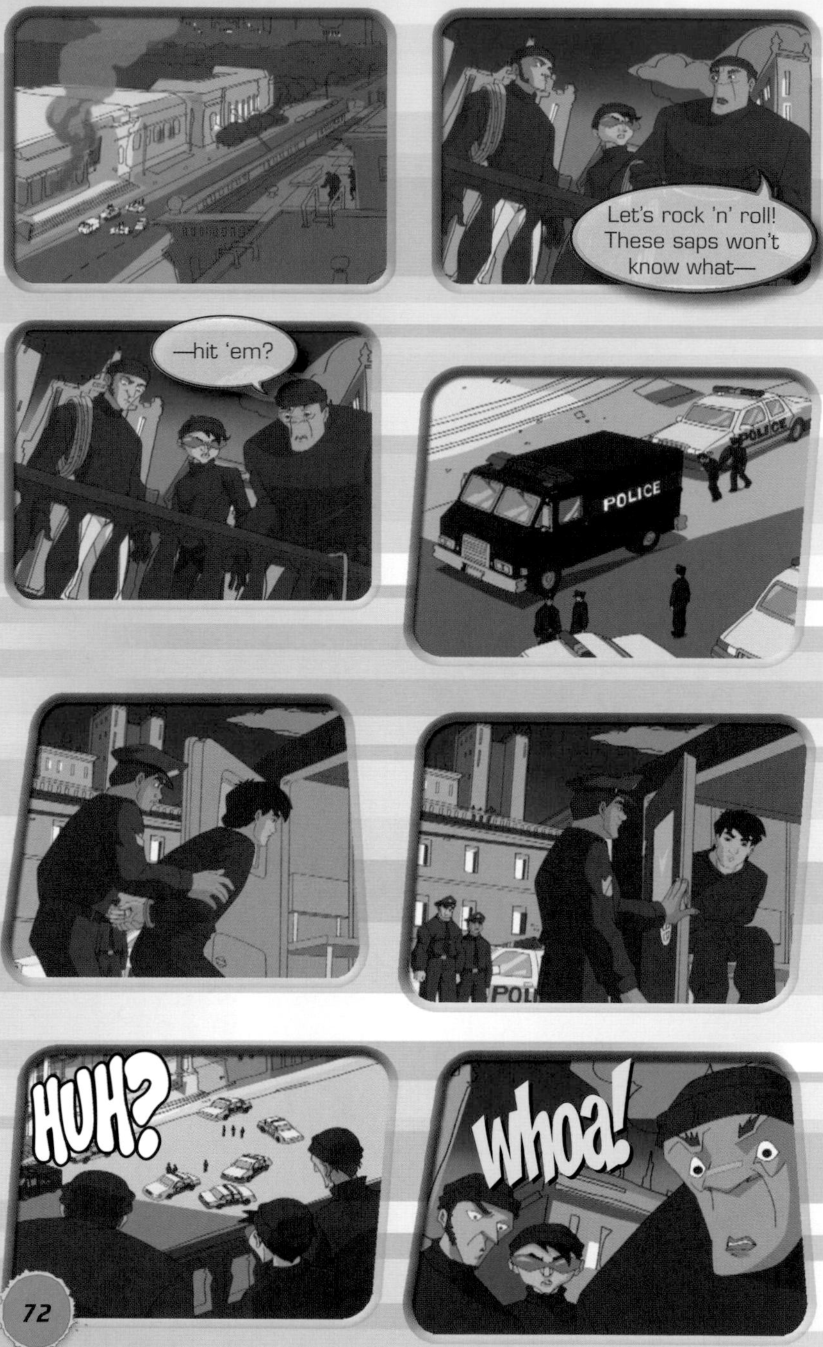
Let's rock 'n' roll! These saps won't know what—
—hit 'em?
POLICE
POLI
HUH?
whoa!

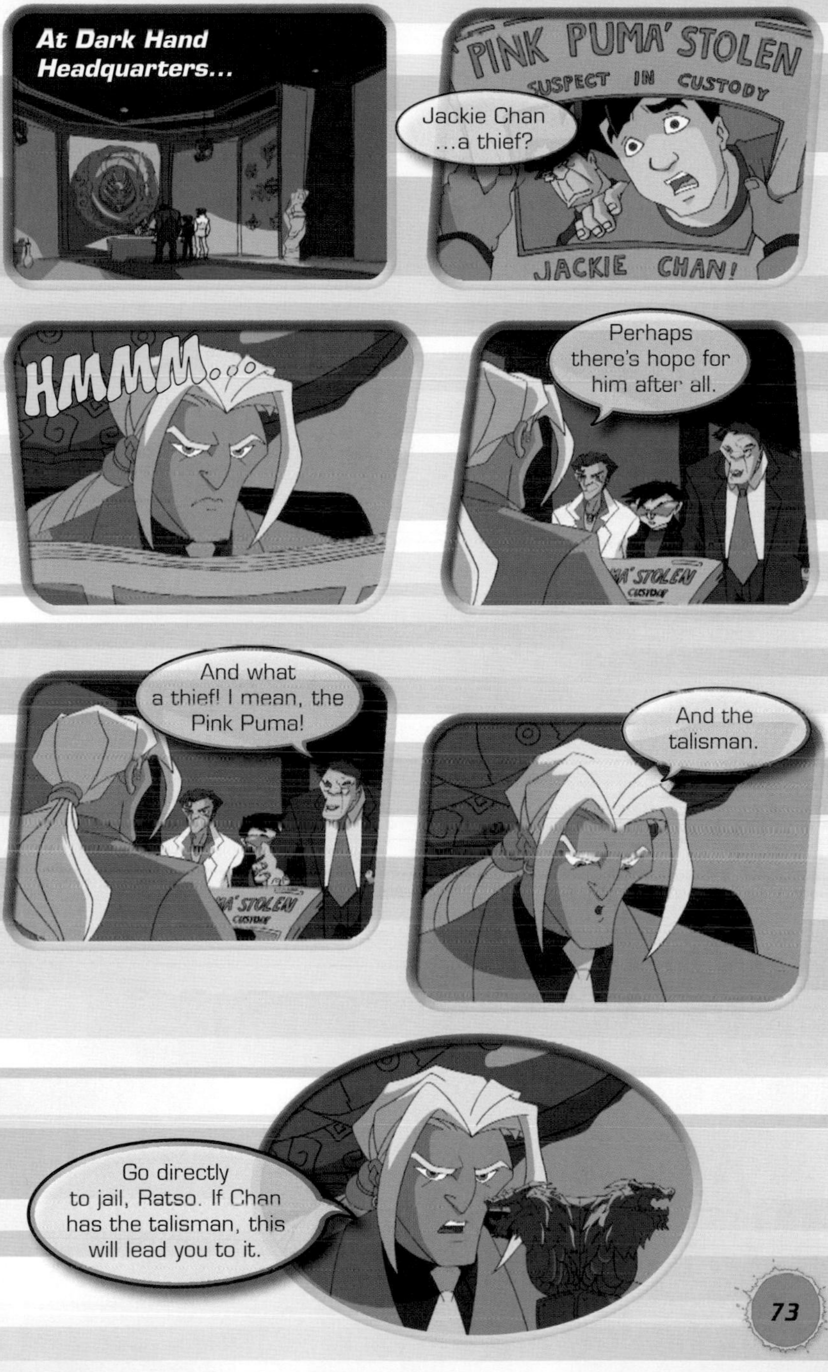
At Dark Hand Headquarters...
PINK PUMA' STOLEN
SUSPECT IN CUSTODY
JACKIE CHAN!
Jackie Chan ...a thief?
HMMM
Perhaps there's hope for him after all.
And what a thief! I mean, the Pink Puma!
And the talisman.
Go directly to jail, Ratso. If Chan has the talisman, this will lead you to it.

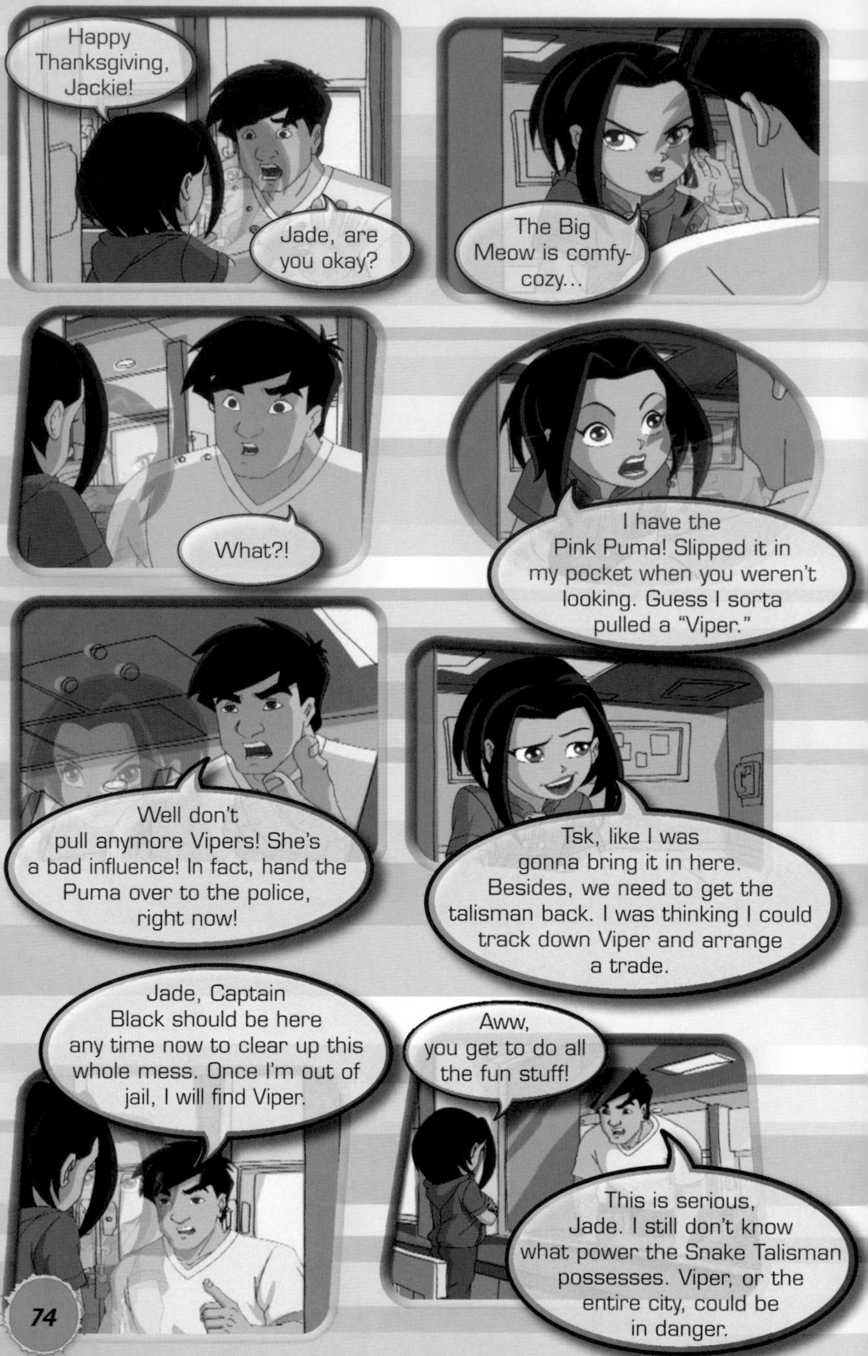
Happy Thanksgiving, Jackie!
Jade, are you okay?
The Big Meow is comfy-cozy...
What?!
I have the Pink Puma! Slipped it in my pocket when you weren't looking. Guess I sorta pulled a "Viper."
Well don't pull anymore Vipers! She's a bad influence! In fact, hand the Puma over to the police, right now!
Tsk, like I was gonna bring it in here. Besides, we need to get the talisman back. I was thinking I could track down Viper and arrange a trade.
Jade, Captain Black should be here any time now to clear up this whole mess. Once I'm out of jail, I will find Viper.
Aww, you get to do all the fun stuff!
This is serious, Jade. I still don't know what power the Snake Talisman possesses. Viper, or the entire city, could be in danger.

At Viper's penthouse apartment...

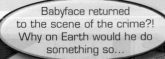

Babyface returned to the scene of the crime?! Why on Earth would he do something so...

...stupid.

GASP!

What am I supposed to do with this?!

Whoa.

HSSSS

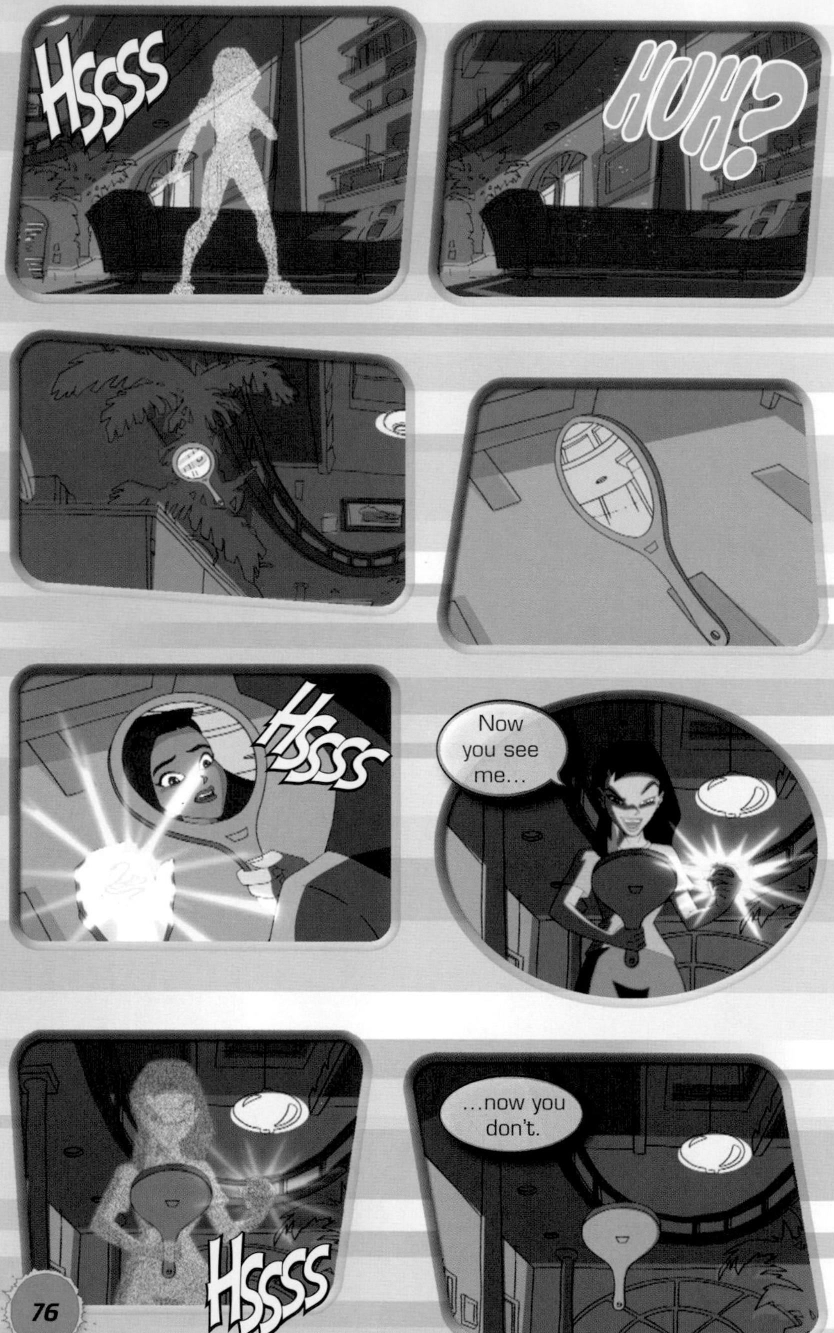
HSSSS
HUH?
HSSSS
Now you see me...
HSSSS
...now you don't.

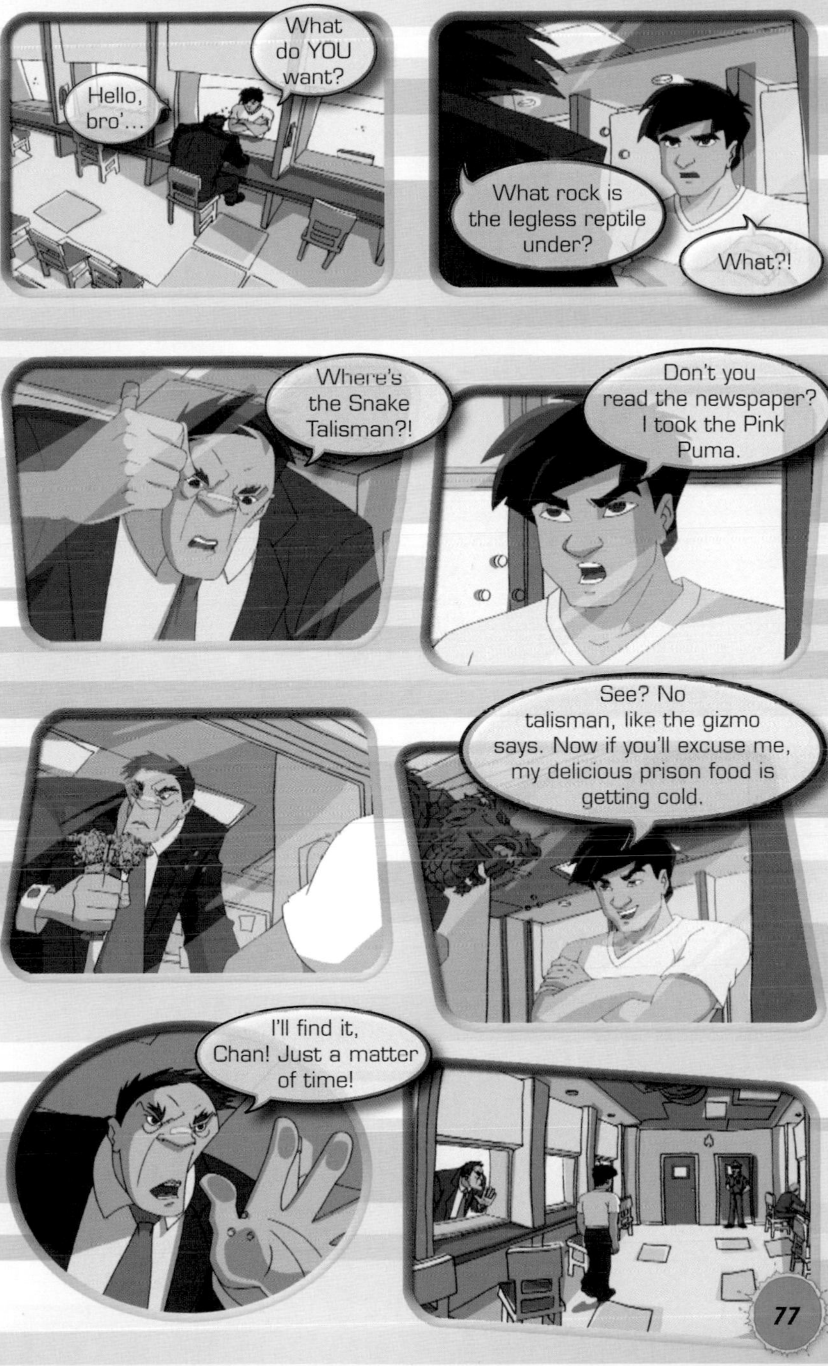
Hello, bro'...
What do YOU want?
What rock is the legless reptile under?
What?!
Where's the Snake Talisman?!
Don't you read the newspaper? I took the Pink Puma.
See? No talisman, like the gizmo says. Now if you'll excuse me, my delicious prison food is getting cold.
I'll find it, Chan! Just a matter of time!

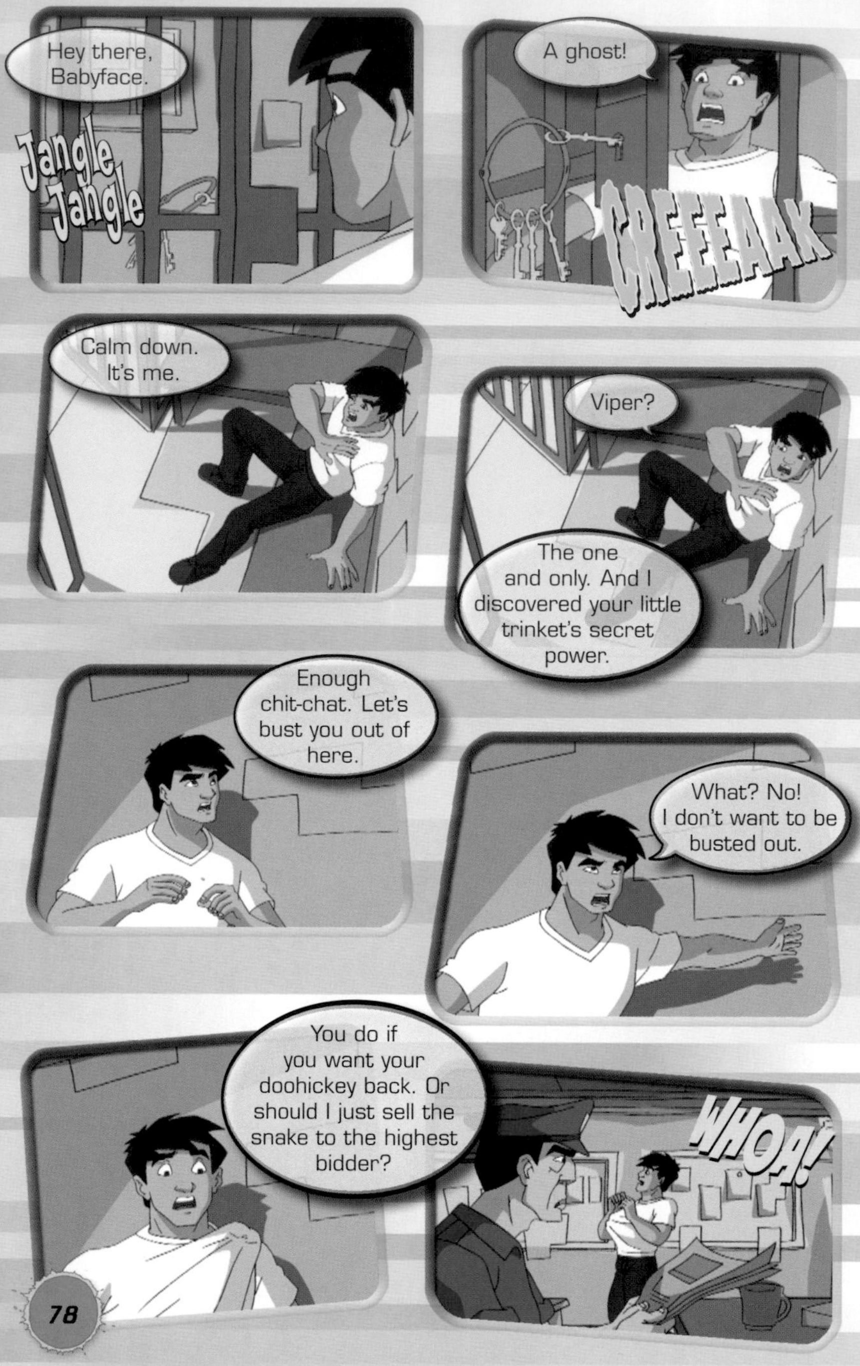
Hey there, Babyface.
Jangle Jangle
A ghost!
CREEEAAK
Calm down. It's me.
Viper?
The one and only. And I discovered your little trinket's secret power.
Enough chit-chat. Let's bust you out of here.
What? No! I don't want to be busted out.
You do if you want your doohickey back. Or should I just sell the snake to the highest bidder?
WHOA!

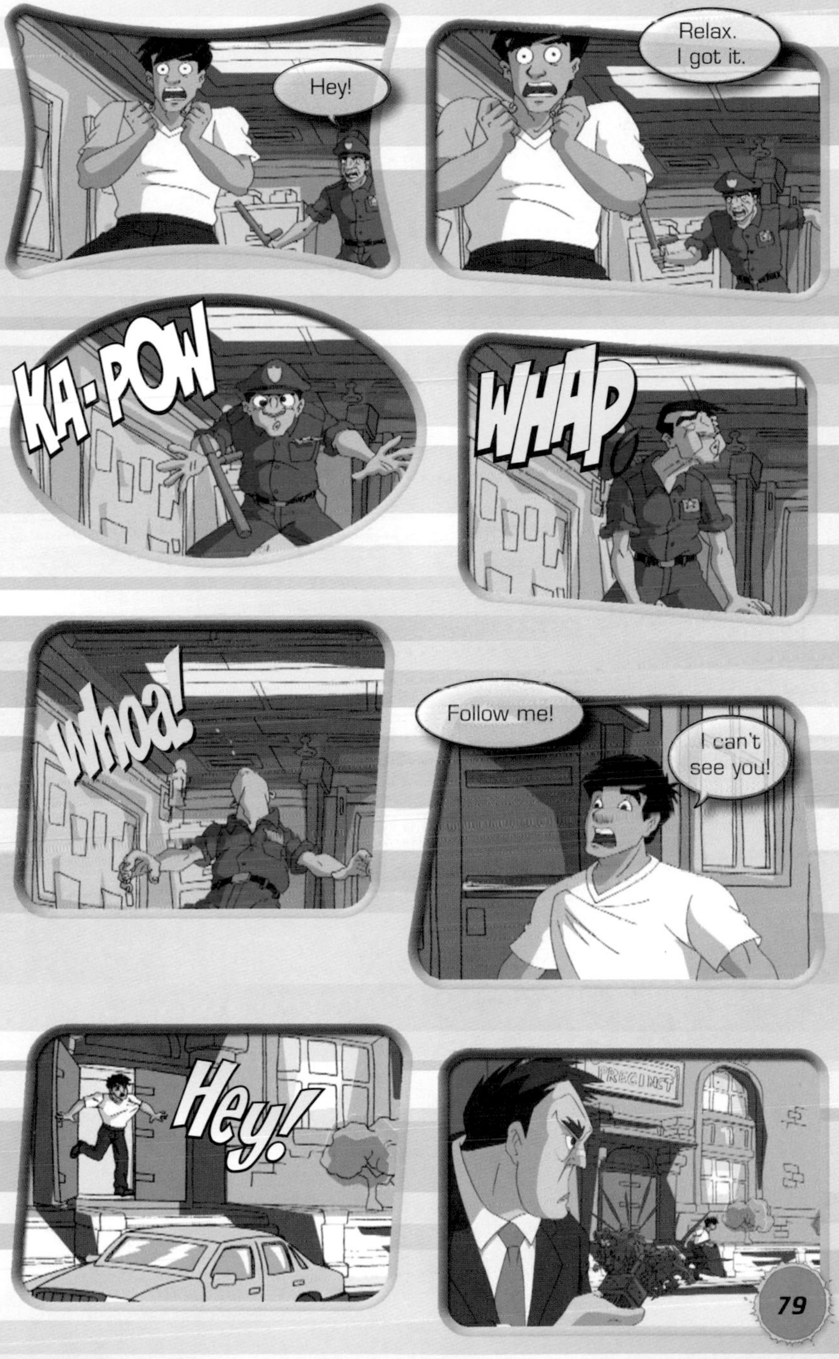
Hey!
Relax.
I got it.
KA-POW
WHAP
Whoa!
Follow me!
I can't see you!
Hey!
PRECINCT

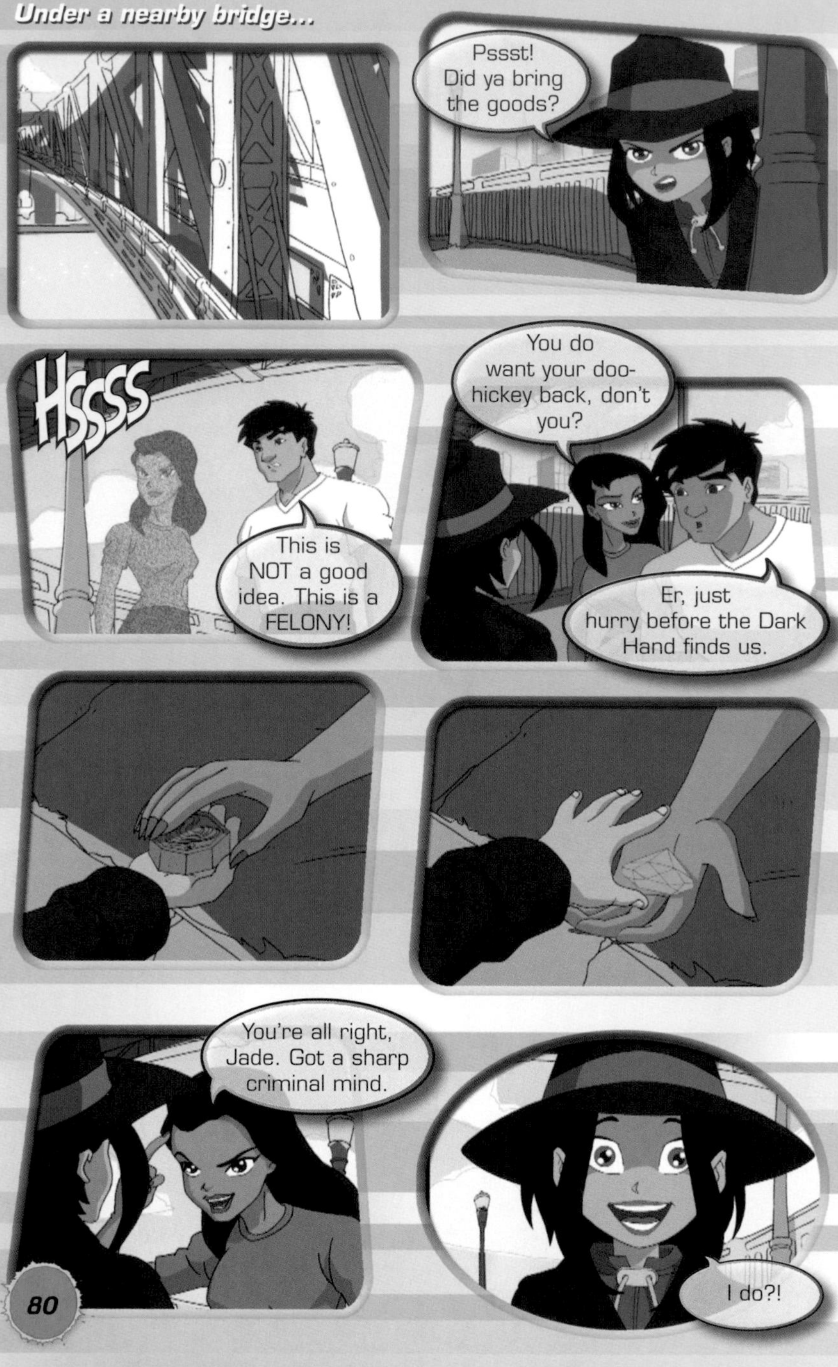
Under a nearby bridge...
Pssst! Did ya bring the goods?
HSSSS
This is NOT a good idea. This is a FELONY!
You do want your doo-hickey back, don't you?
Er, just hurry before the Dark Hand finds us.
You're all right, Jade. Got a sharp criminal mind.
I do?!

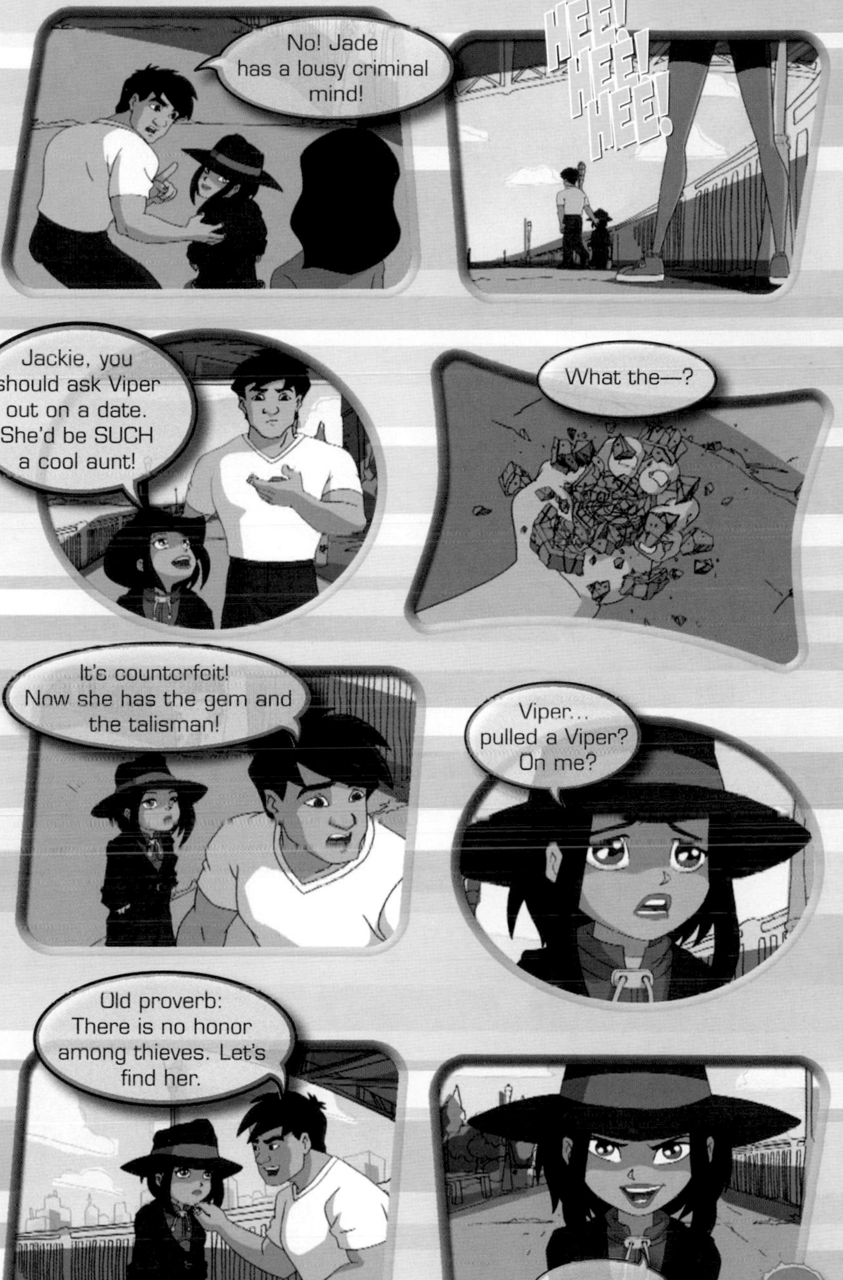
No! Jade has a lousy criminal mind!
HEE! HEE! HEE!
Jackie, you should ask Viper out on a date. She'd be SUCH a cool aunt!
What the—?
It's counterfeit! Now she has the gem and the talisman!
Viper... pulled a Viper? On me?
Old proverb: There is no honor among thieves. Let's find her.
Let's!

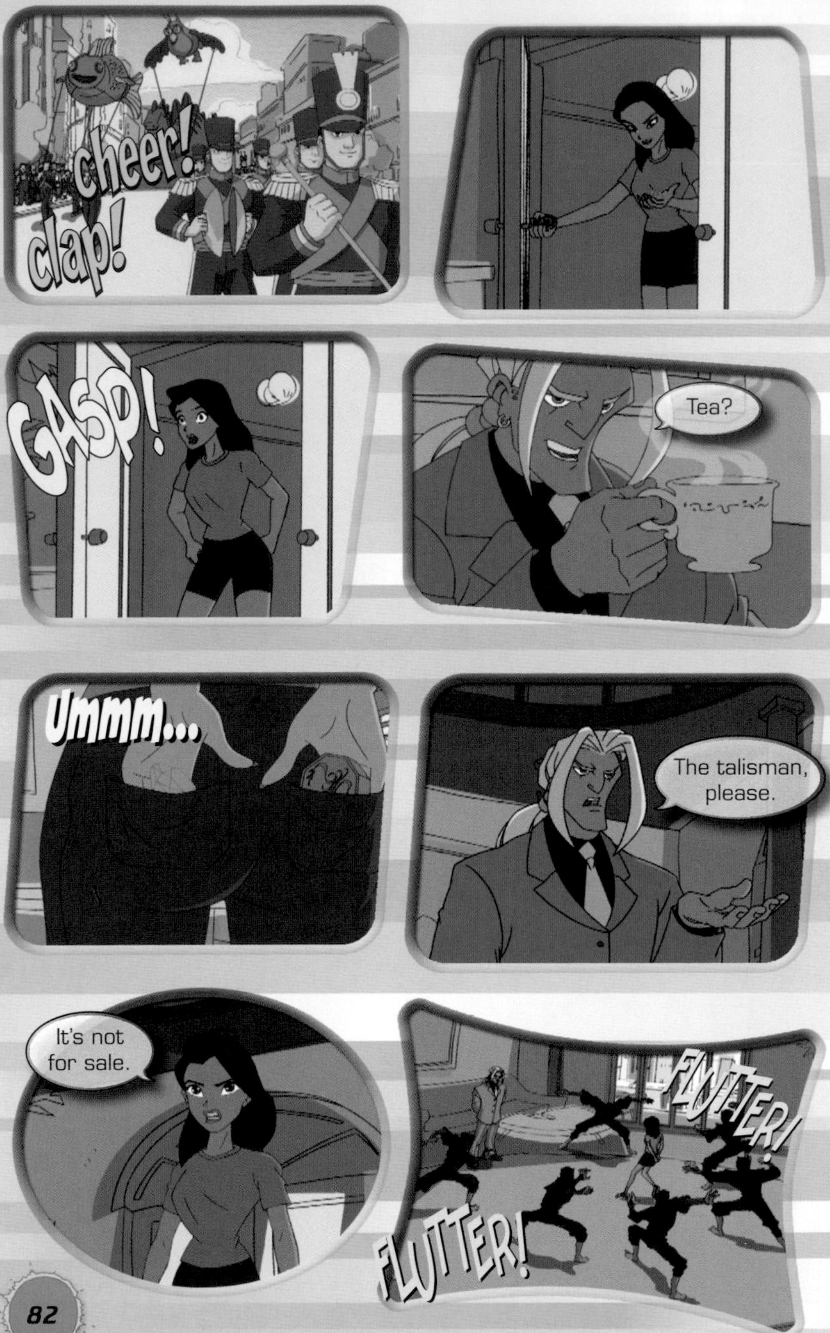
cheer!
clap!
GASP!
Tea?
Ummm...
The talisman, please.
It's not for sale.
FLUTTER!
FLUTTER!

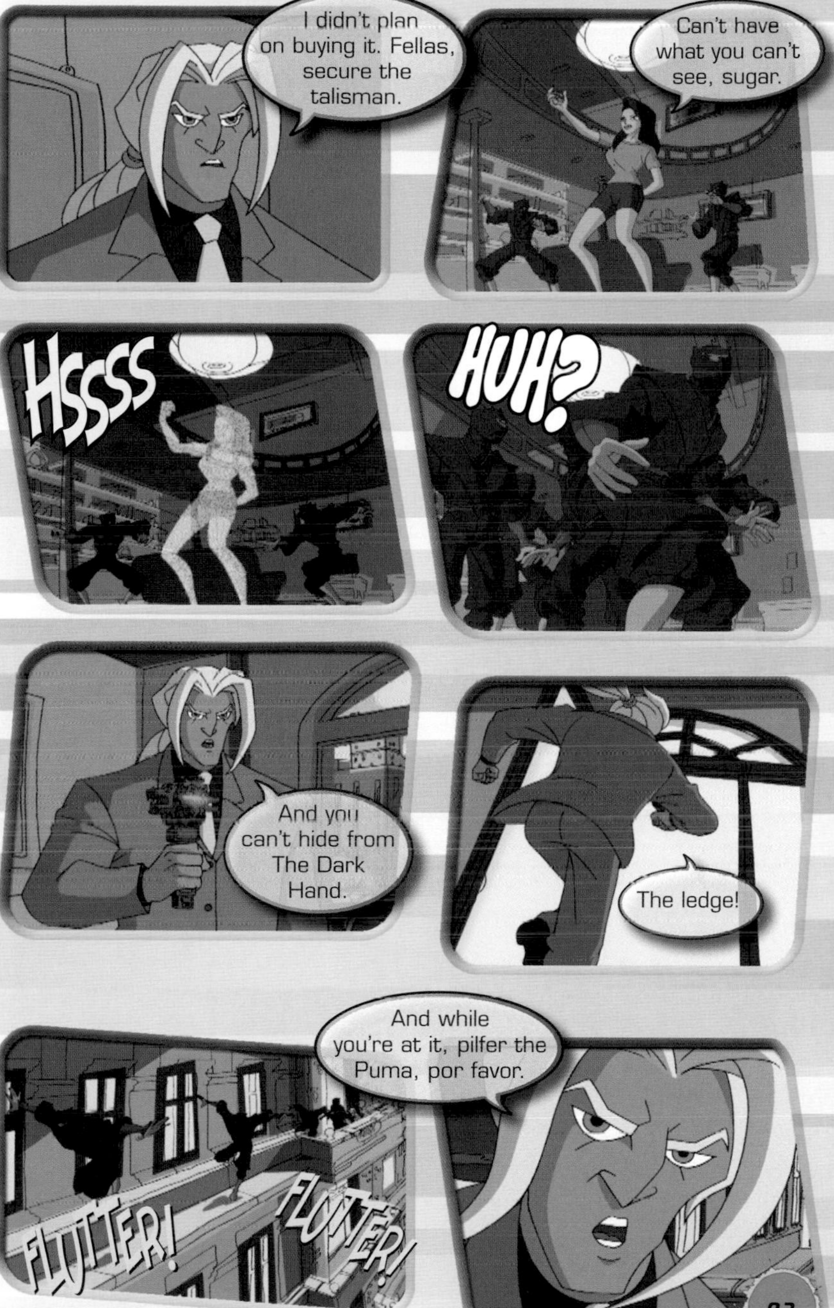
I didn't plan on buying it. Fellas, secure the talisman.
Can't have what you can't see, sugar.
HSSSS
HUH?
And you can't hide from The Dark Hand.
The ledge!
And while you're at it, pilfer the Puma, por favor.
FLUTTER!
FLUTTER!

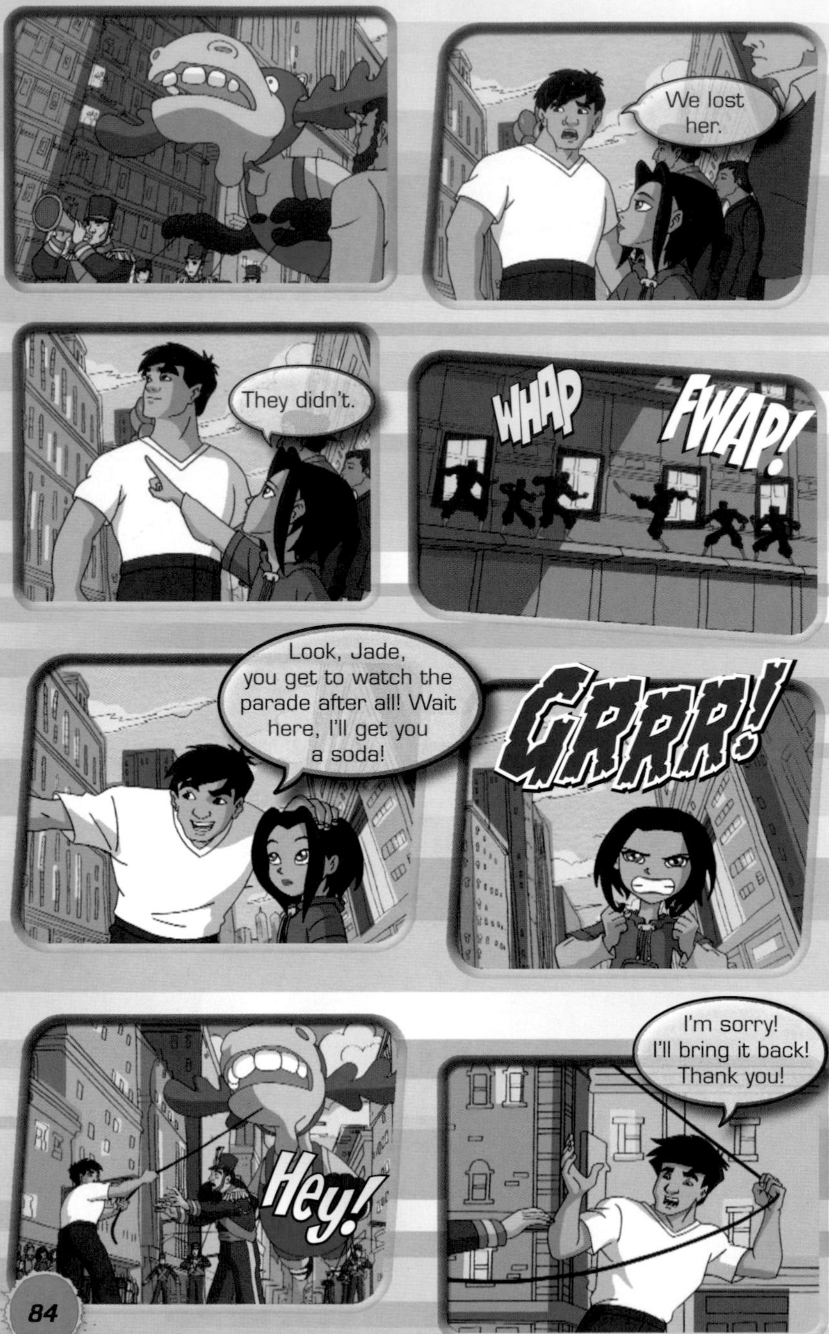
We lost her.
They didn't.
WHAP
FWAP!
Look, Jade, you get to watch the parade after all! Wait here, I'll get you a soda!
GRRR!
Hey!
I'm sorry! I'll bring it back! Thank you!

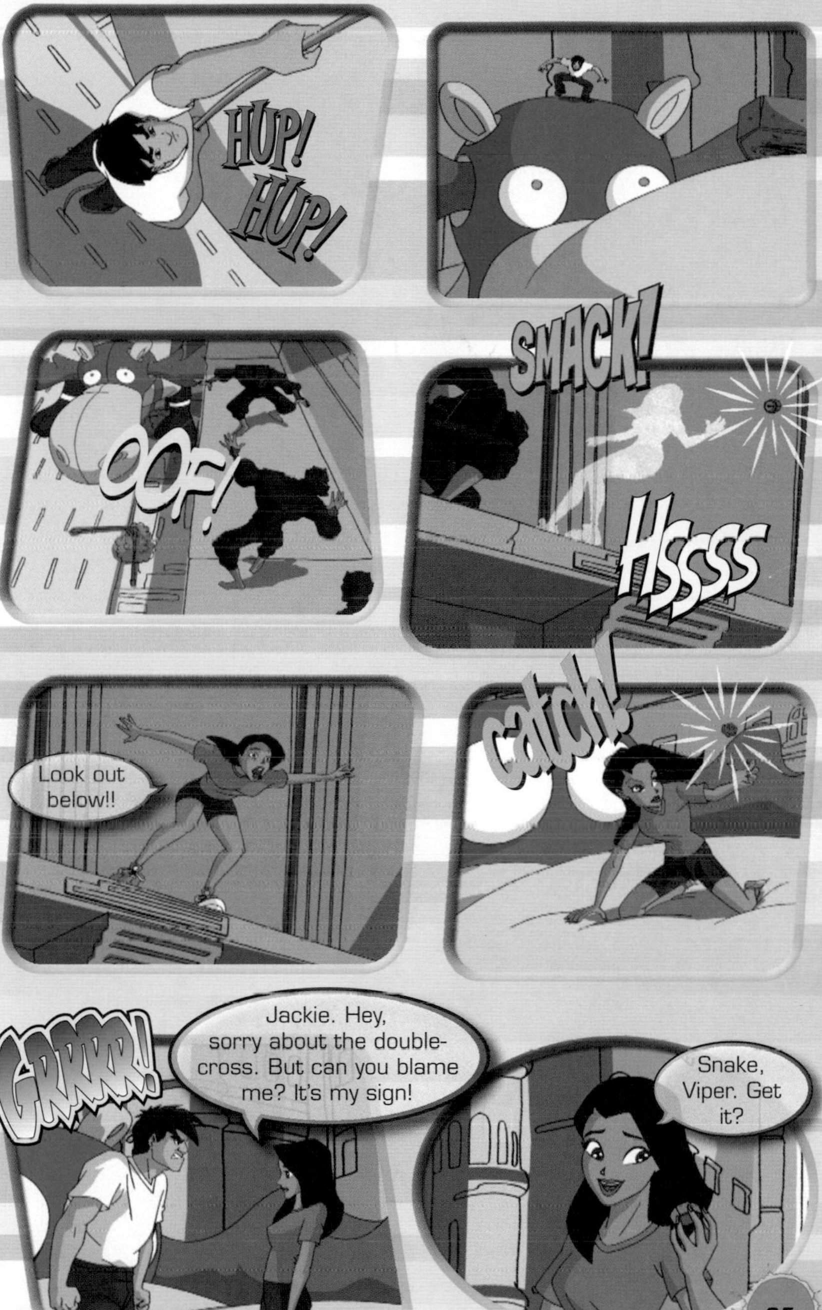
HUP!
HUP!
OOF!
SMACK!
HSSSS
Look out below!!
catch!
GRRRR!
Jackie. Hey, sorry about the double-cross. But can you blame me? It's my sign!
Snake, Viper. Get it?

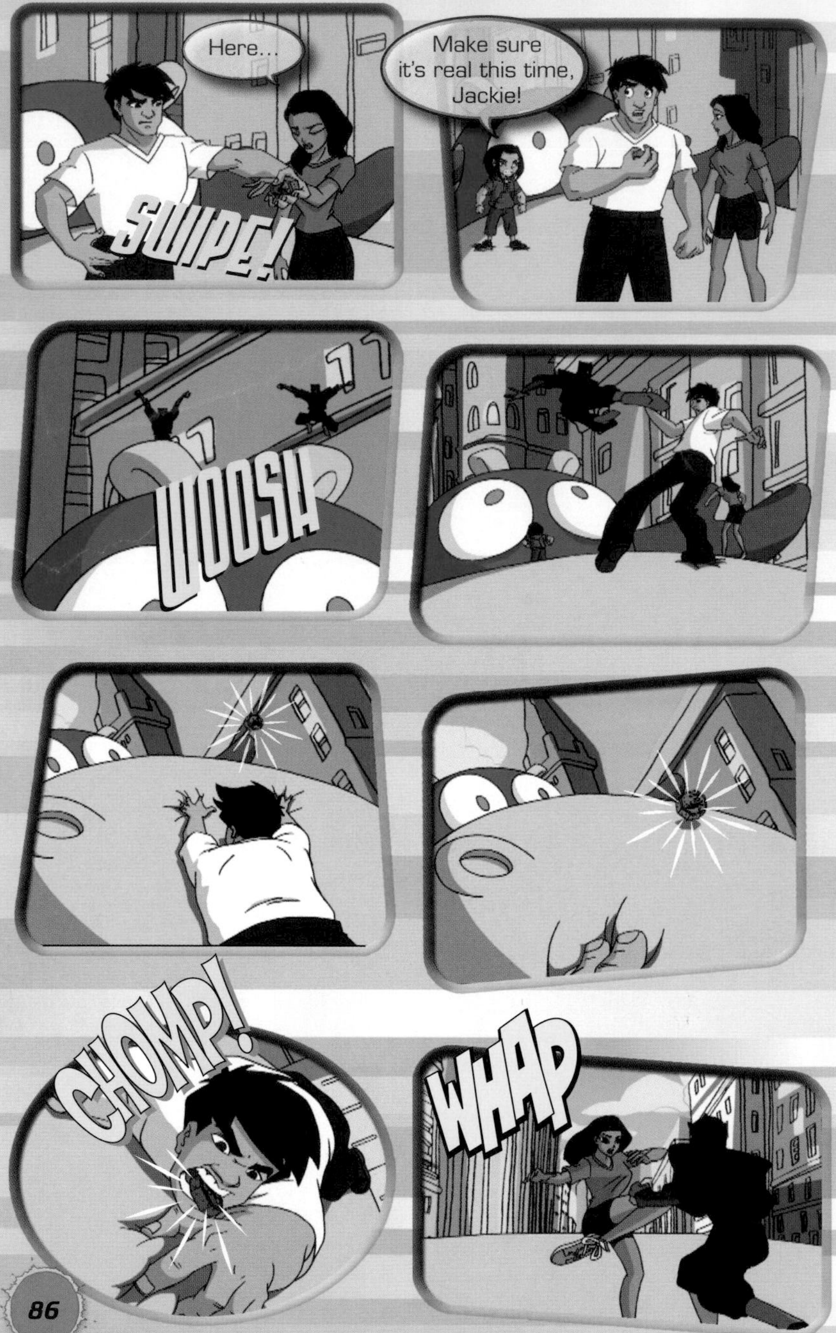
Here...
SWIPE!
Make sure it's real this time, Jackie!
WOOSH
CHOMP!
WHAP

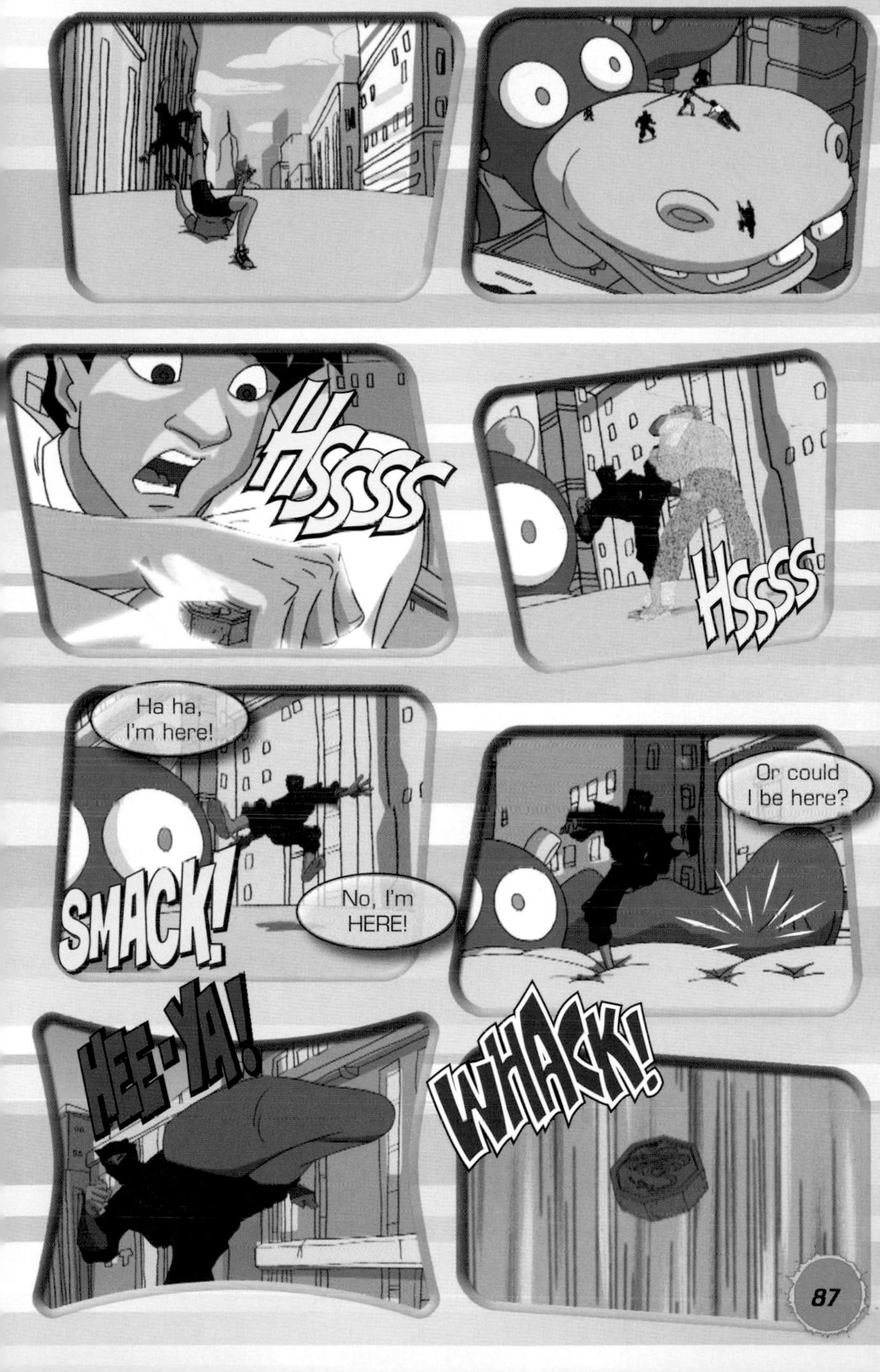
HSSSS
HSSSS
Ha ha, I'm here!
SMACK!
No, I'm HERE!
Or could I be here?
HEE-YA!
WHACK!

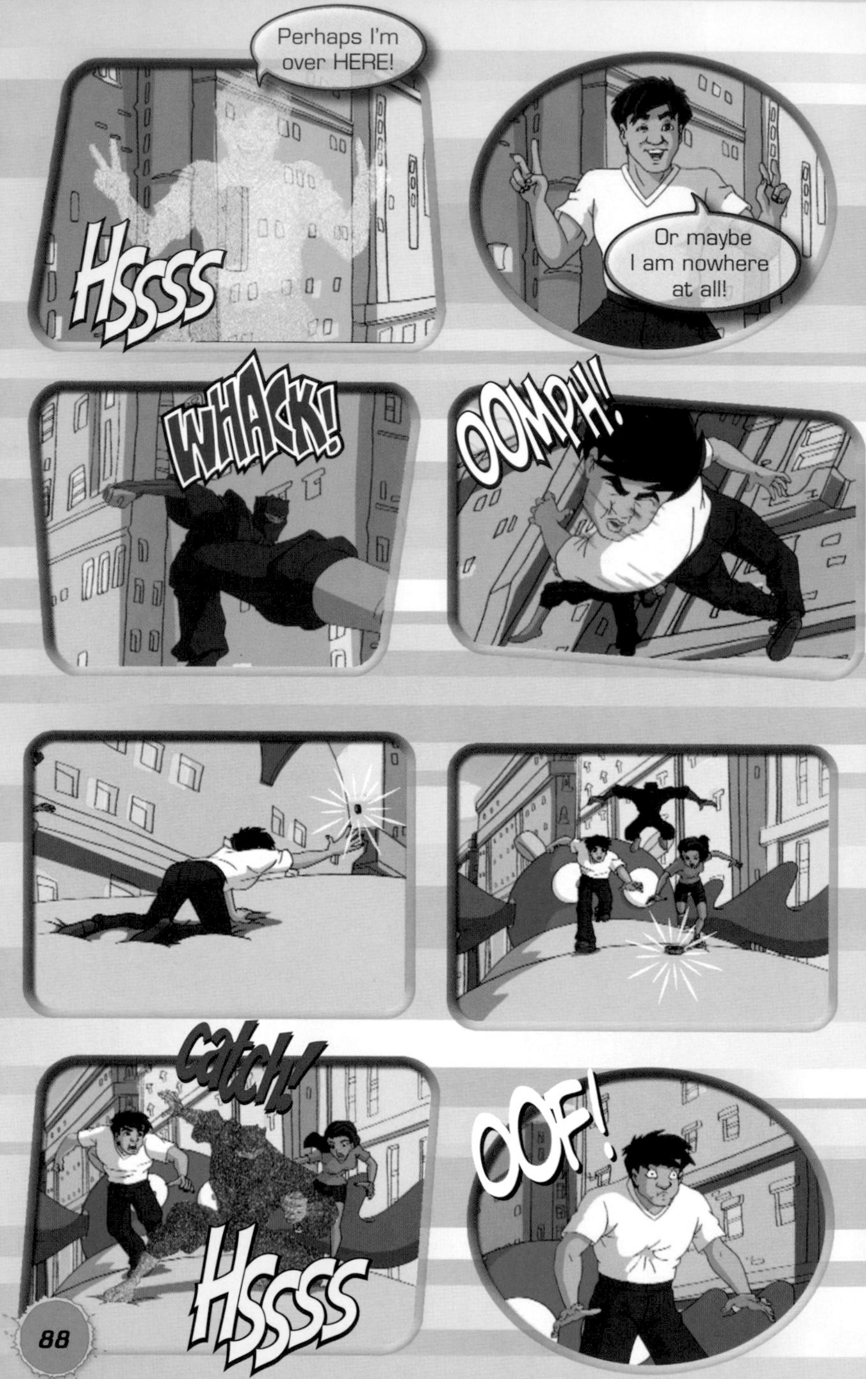
Perhaps I'm over HERE!
HSSSS
Or maybe I am nowhere at all!
WHACK!
OOMPH!
catch!
HSSSS
OOF!

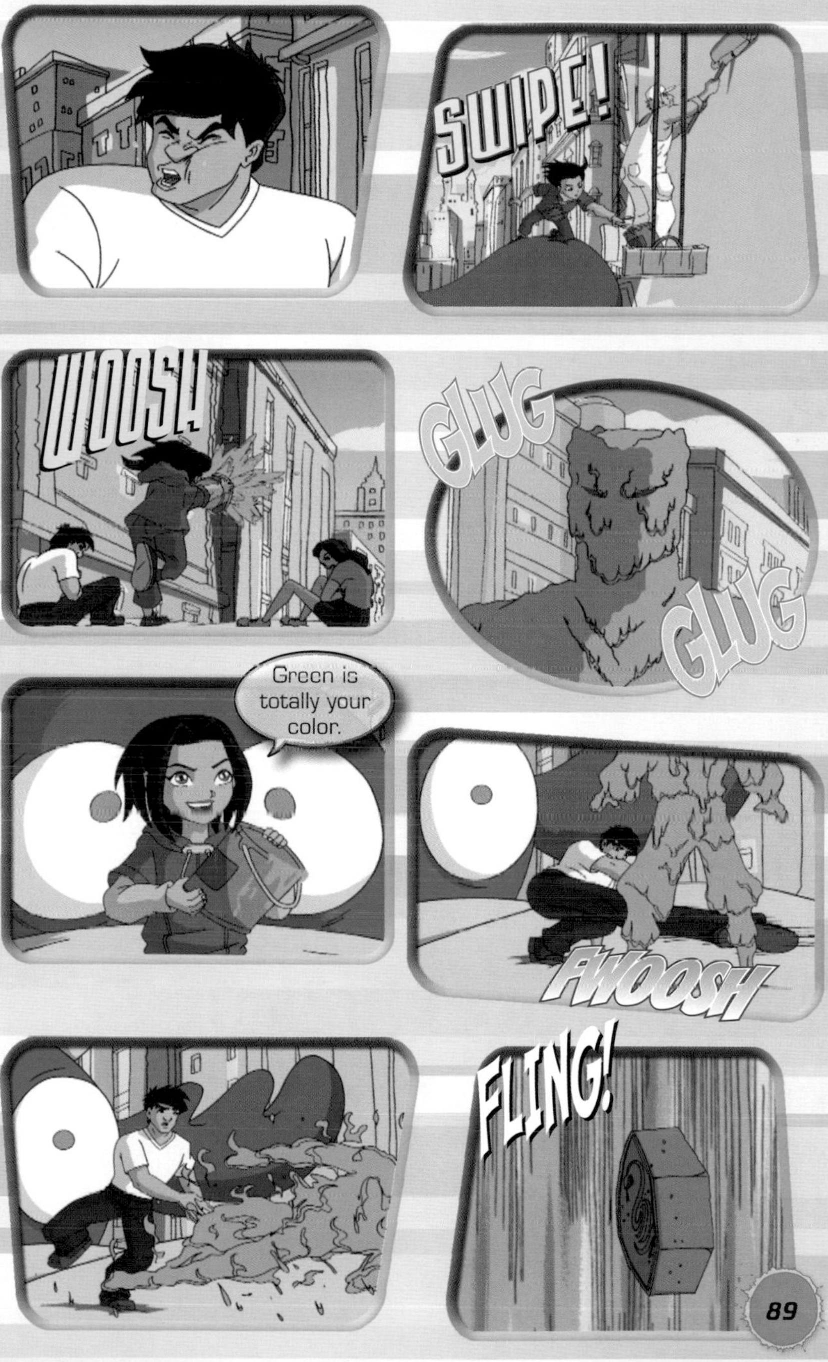
SWIPE!
WOOSH
GLUG
GLUG
Green is totally your color.
FWOOSH
FLING!

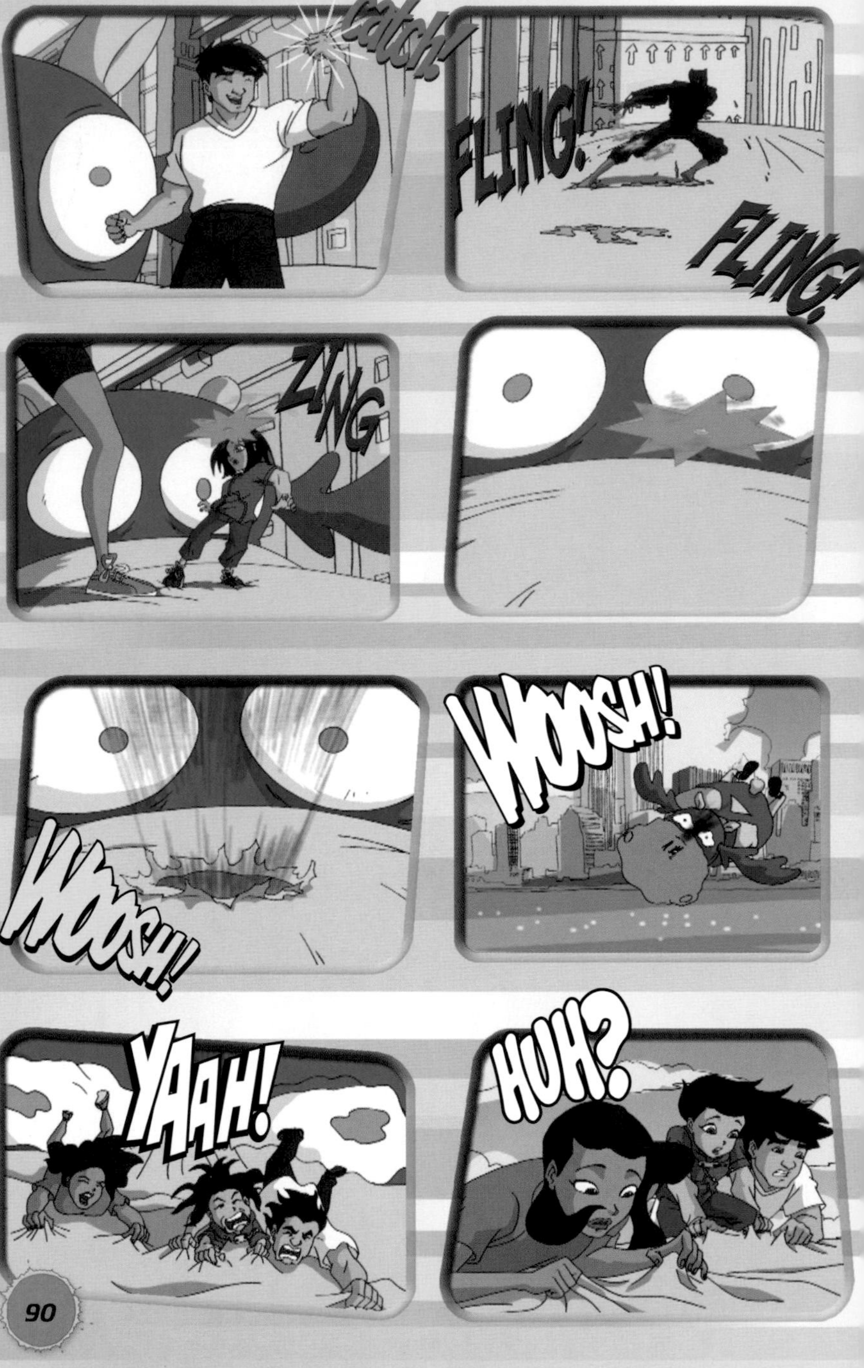
catch!
FLING!
FLING!
ZING
WOOSH!
WOOSH!
YAAH!
HUH?

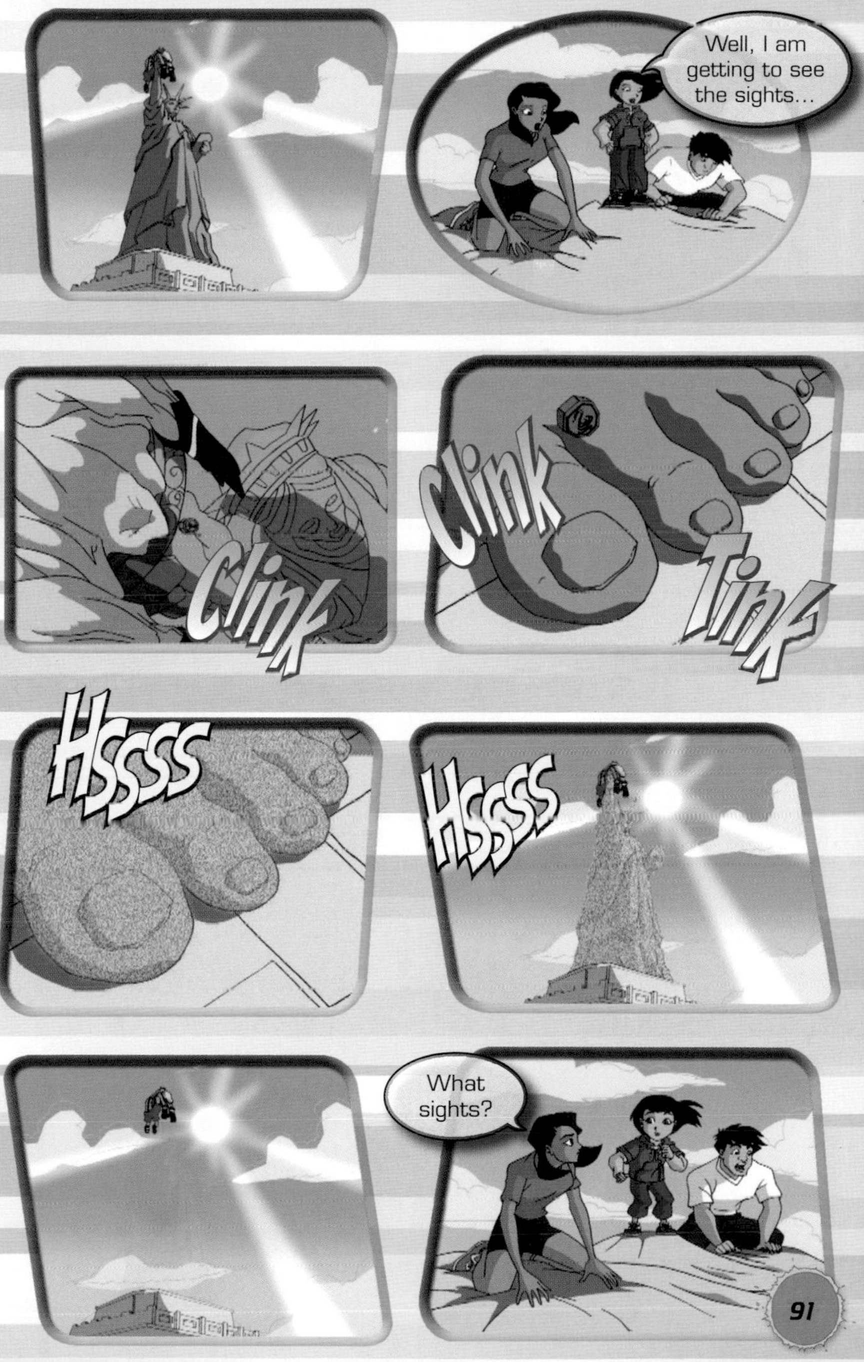
Well, I am getting to see the sights...
Clink
Clink
Tink
Hssss
Hssss
What sights?

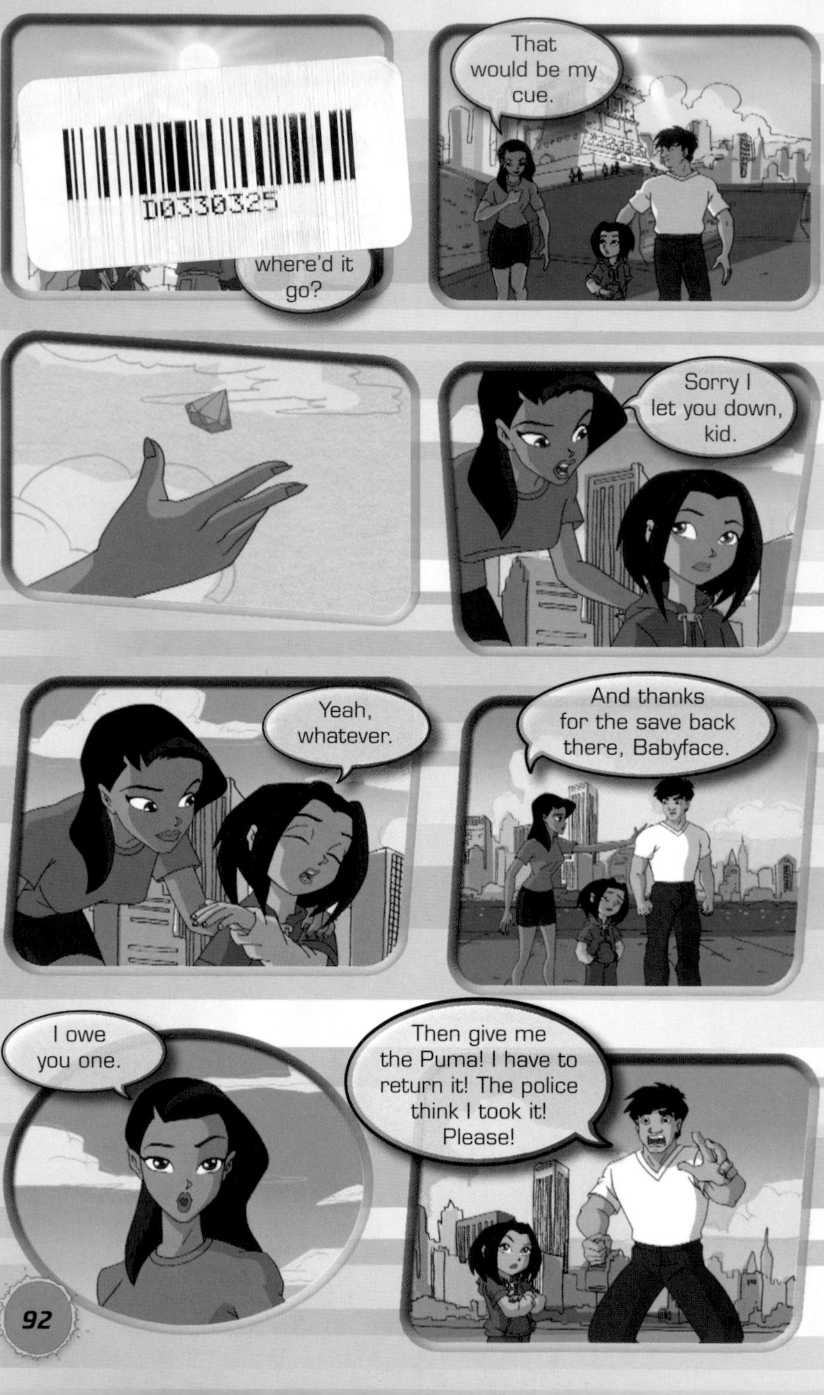
where'd it go?
That would be my cue.
Sorry I let you down, kid.
Yeah, whatever.
And thanks for the save back there, Babyface.
I owe you one.
Then give me the Puma! I have to return it! The police think I took it! Please!

ALSO AVAILABLE FROM ⊙ TOKYOPOP®

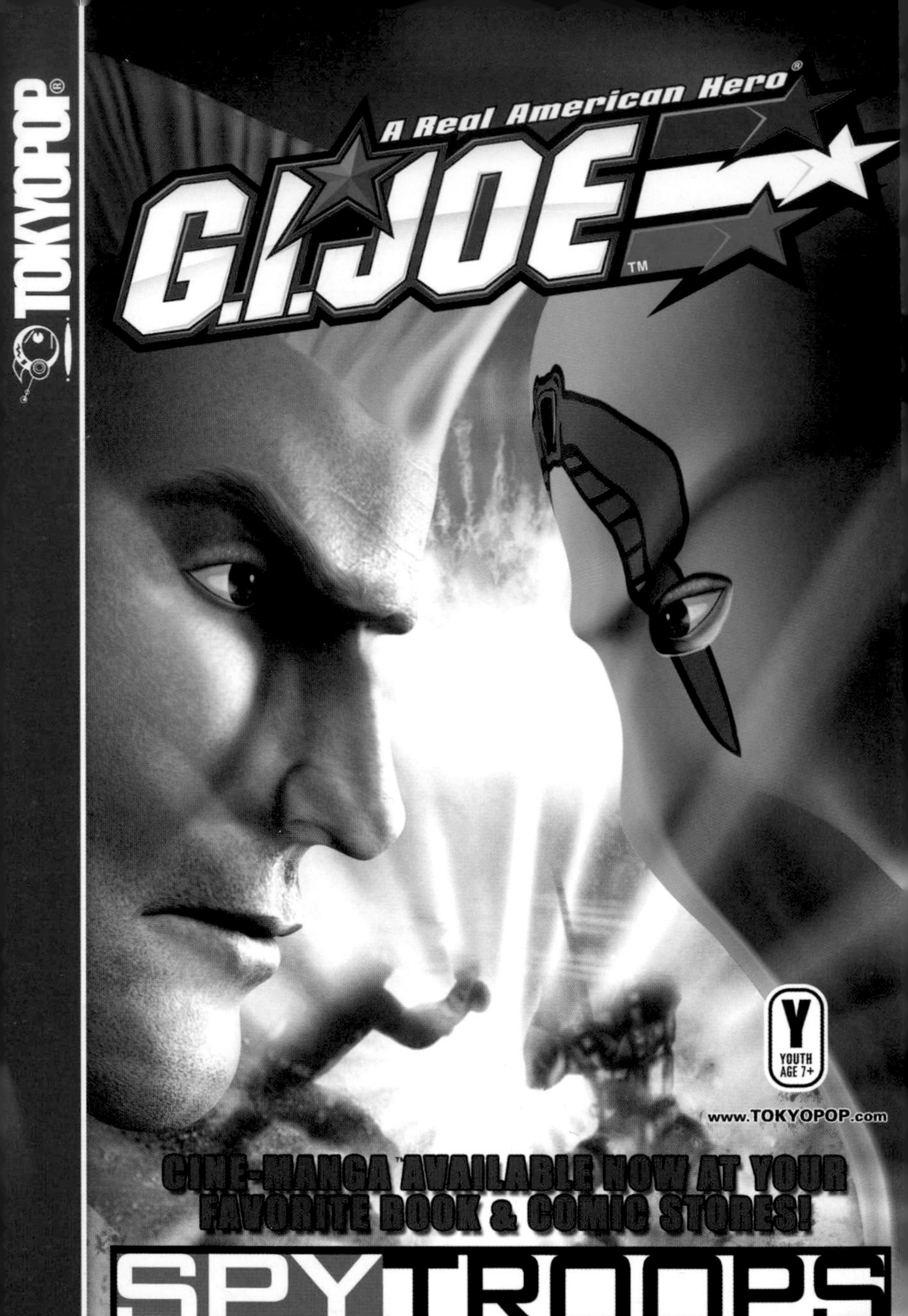
TOKYOPOP®
A Real American Hero®
G.I. JOE™
Y
YOUTH AGE 7+
www.TOKYOPOP.com
CINE-MANGA™ AVAILABLE NOW AT YOUR FAVORITE BOOK & COMIC STORES!
SPY TROOPS